FBI SECRETS

Advance Praise for FBI SECRETS by M. Wesley Swearingen

"FBI SECRETS ought to snap Americans out of their complacency over this covert agency. It rips aside the curtain hiding bigotry, burglary, and accessory to murder, setting up what should be a Bureaugate."
  –William W. Turner, former FBI Special Agent, author of *Hoover's FBI: The Men and the Myth*

"A former insider's guided tour of the FBI's chamber of horrors, documenting in shocking detail crimes ranging from bag jobs to sanctioned assassinations, FBI SECRETS is a must read for anyone concerned with the subversion of the democratic process."
  –Curt Gentry, author of *J. Edgar Hoover: The Man and the Secrets*

"At last, an FBI whistleblower! Here is the inside story of FBI break-ins and the frame-up of Black Panther leader Geronimo Pratt. Must reading for '60s veterans, today's activists, and anyone who values freedom and democracy."
  –Brian Glick, legal counsel to Geronimo Pratt and author of *War at Home*

"With this book, Wes Swearingen does for the FBI what Philip Agee did for the CIA. In clear, eye-witness detail, he exposes the day-to-day corruption and subversion of democratic values that has permeated our national police since its inception, and which continues to this day."
  –William H. Schaap, co-founder, *CovertAction Quarterly*

"Swearingen skewers Hoover with this *film noire* account of corruption, racism and authoritarianism among the G-Men of the FBI. As fiction it would be a classic, but as fact it is a powerful tragedy detailing how ultra-patriotism and power breed repression and police-state mentality."
  –Chip Berlet, co-chair, Civil Liberties Committee, National Lawyers Guilde

F B I   S E C R E T S

An Agent's Exposé

By M. Wesley Swearingen

South End Press   Boston, MA

Text design and production by the South End Press collective

Library of Congress Cataloging-in-Publication Data
Swearingen, M. Wesley
FBI Secrets: an agent's exposé/ M. Wesley Swearingen [i.e. Swearingen]
    p. cm.
Includes bibliographic references and index.
    ISBN 0-89608-502-3: $40.00. —ISBN 0-89608-501-5 (pbk.): $13.00
    1. Swearingen, M. Wesley. 2. United States. Federal Bureau of Investigation—Officials and employees—Biography. 3. United States. Federal Bureau of Investigation. 4. Political persecution—United States—Case studies. I. Title.
    HV7911.S844A3   1995
    363.2'5'0973—dc20   94-39629

                                                    CIP
South End Press, 116 Saint Botolph Street, Boston, MA 02115
99 98 97 96 95   ® GCIU ~   1 2 3 4 5 6 7 8

To the memory of my dear friend, Charles R. Garry, who spent his life in the courtroom in the struggle for human rights and human dignity for all.

Acknowledgements

I owe thanks to my attorney, Charles R. Garry, who convinced me that my story should be heard by the people, to help them in their struggle for equal rights under the law, and who helped me on my way to exposing FBI corruption.

I wish to thank John Crewdson, former reporter for the *New York Times* and currently national editor of the *Chicago Tribune*, for writing accurate news articles about FBI corruption based on my information, and for encouraging me to publish my memoirs.

I want to express my gratitude to the South End Press collective for having the courage to publish an agent's first-hand account of FBI corruption and wrongdoing. Loie Hayes deserves a commendation for supporting my early drafts, and for having faith in a first-time author. My editor, Sonia Shah, is the one who made it all possible because she had to edit out many personal stories, anecdotes, and sidelines to keep the book focused on the story line.

Contents

"There is something addicting about a secret."
—J. Edgar Hoover (1895-1972)

F o r e w o r d

Lifting the Shroud of Secrecy
by Ward Churchill

During the ten years that I was on the U.S. Intelligence Board...never once did I hear anybody, including myself, raise the questions: "Is this course of action which we have agreed upon lawful, is it legal, is it moral and ethical?" We never gave any thought to that realm of reasoning, because we were just naturally pragmatists. The one thing we were concerned with was this: Will this course of action work, will it get us what we want, will it reach the objective we desire to reach?

-William C. Sullivan, former FBI Assistant Director,
Domestic Intelligence Division

Beginning with the 1971 citizens' break-in at the Media, Pennsylvania Resident Agency FBI office, in which a large number of Top Secret documents were stolen and subsequently made public, the past quarter-century has been replete with revelations concerning pervasive criminal activities engaged in by the Federal Bureau of Investigation.[1] Over the years, it has become increasingly apparent that such conduct on the part of the "nation's police force" has, overwhelmingly, been directed against politically dissident individuals and organizations. This is how the bureau has functioned from its inception in 1908 to today. In effect, the FBI exists, as much as anything else, as a national political police.

Much of the operational history of the bureau's many campaigns against political diversity in the United States has been detailed in the voluminous reports of a Senate Select Committee (Church Committee) during the mid-70s,[2] and in such books as

i

Robert Justin Goldstein's *Political Repression in Modern America*, Cathy Perkus' *COINTELPRO*, Athan Theoharis' *Spying on Americans*, David Wise's *The American Police State*, Peter Matthiessen's *In the Spirit of Crazy Horse*, Brian Glick's *War at Home*, David Garrow's *The FBI and Martin Luther King, Jr.*, Ross Gelbspan's *Break-ins, Death Threats and the FBI*, and my own collaborations with Jim VanderWall, *Agents of Repression* and *The COINTELPRO Papers*.[3]

From this array of sources, both primary and secondary, emerges a portrait of a massive, deeply entrenched and increasingly ubiquitous institutional entity devoted to the curtailment of domestic political action and expression. The individual objects of the bureau's attentions in this respect have been people as different in their lives and outlooks as Ernest Hemingway and Dr. Martin Luther King, Jr., the Berrigan brothers and Russell Means, Bernardine Dohrn and Malcolm X, Janis Joplin and Kathy Boudin, Huey P. Newton and Joan Baez, George Jackson and Walter Reuther. The organizations subject to FBI counterintelligence operations have been equally wide-ranging, extending from the Black Panther Party, American Indian Movement, Puerto Rican *independentistas* and the Weathermen faction of the Students for a Democratic Society, to the entirety of the labor movement and the Communist and Socialist Workers parties, and onward still, to the Student Nonviolent Coordinating Committee, Committee in Solidarity with the People of El Salvador (CISPES), Every Mother for Peace, Clergy and Laity Concerned, Silo Plowshares, even Duke University.[4]

On record, the methods employed against such "deviants" have included every sort of tactic from discrediting targeted persons or groups by circulating defamatory rumors about them in their communities and/or planting false reports about them in the media, to causing "politically objectionable individuals" to be evicted from their homes and fired from their jobs by contacting their landlords and employers, to orchestrating the repeated arrests on spurious charges of those targeted, to obtaining the conviction and consequent imprisonment of "key activists" by introducing fabricated evidence against them at trial, to provoking inter- and intragroup violence, to outright assassination of selected leaders.[5] Although the profile of the FBI's lexicon of illicitly repressive modes and methods is in some ways substantially complete, there has always been an important missing ingredient: namely, detailed tales of the bureau's adventures and wrongdoings. In contrast, much has been written about the activities of the Central Intelligence Agency (CIA), the FBI's figurative counterpart in U.S. external affairs. Several former CIA agents and officials have offered up details that corroborate and amplify the information about CIA techniques available from official and unofficial sources.[6] The dramatic stories of Philip Agee, John Stockwell, Victor Marchetti, Frank Snepp, and Ralph McGehee have clarified and confirmed our knowledge of "The Company."[7]

Unfortunately, it seems the bureau has produced virtually nobody—until now—with the requisite conscience, courage, and personal integrity to match their CIA counterparts in disclosing their insider's direct knowledge of what the FBI has done. Indeed, the major example of an agent who "quit and told" has until now been Joseph Schott, whose 1975 book, *No Left Turns*, was designed to embarrass the memory of FBI Director J. Edgar Hoover.[8] An earlier effort by former agent William Turner, *Hoover's FBI*, was so limited as to be nearly useless in today's research on the FBI.[9]

Given the veritable vacuum into which it injects itself, then, the present book is not only unique but vitally important. Here at last is a career veteran of the bureau's clandestine wars against political freedom in America—a participant in literally hundreds of burglaries, disinformation campaigns, and worse—who has, however belatedly, demonstrated the fortitude and character necessary to admit, first to himself and then to the rest of us, not just the illegality but the intrinsic *wrongness* of what he did "in service to the bureau." Thus, the author, M. Wesley Swearingen, has finally positioned himself to reveal what he learned in the course of his decades as an active-duty FBI agent.

This, to be sure, is a lot. The chapters which follow are laced with privileged information. Exposed, for example, are the mechanics of how Los Angeles Black Panther leader Geronimo ji Jaga Pratt was railroaded into an ongoing life term in prison by agents with whom the author worked during the early 1970s. Similarly, Swearingen recounts a drinking scene in which another agent, a friend with whom he had long worked in Chicago, confessed the bureau's involvement in the December 1969 assassinations of Illinois Panther leaders Fred Hampton and Mark Clark.[10] Light is also shed on the victimization of others, Jean Seberg and Leonard Peltier among them.[11] Additional vignettes highlight the FBI's more-or-less continuous subversion of "objectionable" electoral candidates, the hyper-reactionary racial and sexual attitudes of the average agent, and much more .

Altogether, *FBI Secrets* serves much the same purpose as Agee's *Inside the Company* or Stockwell's *In Search of Enemies*, providing an indispensable validation of certain conclusions already drawn by independent analysts and researchers.[12]

Swearingen's Los Angeles counterintelligence colleagues also played a role in bringing about the murders of other Panthers—Fred Bennett, for instance, and Frank Diggs, Sandra Lane Pratt, Jimmie Carr, Bunchy Carter, and Jon Huggins—and were probably involved in setting up the 1970 Marin County Courthouse disaster that resulted in the deaths of Jonathan Jackson and several others, while very nearly ending the career of activist/intellectual Angela Davis.[13] Scholars and activists are still debating the question of the bureau's possible participation in orchestrating the assassination of George Jackson in 1971.[14]

The FBI also used street gangs during the late-60s and early-70s as surrogates with which to destroy the Panthers.[15] The Party, of course, is known to have fielded a strong and tentatively viable anti-drug program in many inner cities during that period. The gangs with which the bureau aligned itself, and to which it appears to have extended some sort of criminal immunity as a *quid pro quo*—the Black P. Stone Nation *cum* El Rukn group in Chicago is a salient example—largely went on to become primary drug distributors in their respective localities once the Panthers had been obliterated.[16] The FBI's activities on such matters illuminate the meaning of the Reagan/Bush "War on Drugs" and the present Clinton "Get Tough on Crime" initiative.[17]

FBI Secrets represents a giant step toward lifting the shroud of secrecy under which the bureau has sought to conceal its true malignancy. It stands as a singular testimony, a precedent, one which may quite possibly lay the groundwork for other agents or former agents, with other knowledge and other anecdotes, to step forward to share their own insights and experiences. This is certainly an outcome to be hoped for. But, whether or not such a potential is ever borne out, the material herein cries out to be read in its own right, and its author is deserving of genuine respect for having proven himself courageous enough to have written it.

—Ward Churchill
Boulder, Colorado
October 1994

Introduction

I became a Special Agent for the Federal Bureau of Investigation (FBI) in 1951. I did not know, when I joined, that I would learn the expertise of burglary, or that former Director J. Edgar Hoover would instruct agents to violate extortion and kidnapping laws. I did not know then that FBI agents would plot assassinations of American citizens and put innocent individuals in jail just because their skin is black or because they are Native Americans.

I retired in May 1977, completely disillusioned after more than twenty-five years of service. I suffered through over a year of sleepless nights, countless nightmares, and tortured conversations with family and friends before I took the irreversible step of publicly condemning an organization I once had loved and respected.

Because of the FBI's widespread dishonesty and corruption, by the end of my tenure there I had lost the ability to distinguish between different levels of corruption. In the beginning, when I saw new agents being encouraged to cheat on their examinations, I was shocked. But after twenty years of seeing a whole bureau cheat on Inspectors' examinations, concoct fictitious informants, manufacture phony informant reports, and create false statistics, even the most egregious levels of corruption—when top FBI officials lied to the courts, the Department of Justice, and to the U.S. Congress—no longer shocked me. After witnessing twenty years of FBI wrongdoing, I had accepted it as a means to survive in the bureau. So, when Elmer Pratt, the Los Angeles leader of the Black Panther Party, was framed for murder and sentenced to life in prison in 1972 as a target of COINTELPRO, I saw this wrongdoing as about a two on a scale of one to ten.

Consequently, I did not call the attorney general of the United States or the judge who was trying the case when I learned Pratt was to be framed and imprisoned. Many critics have asked me how I could consciously and willingly violate laws I had sworn to uphold. I was a young overzealous patriot, a real "Yankee Doodle Dandy" who loved his country. I was a dangerous person to have in public service because when there appeared to be a threat to our government, I placed the other agents and myself above the law. We did what we thought was good for the country. The other agents and I were the epitome of American naval hero Commodore Stephen Decatur, who said in 1816, "Our country, right or wrong." Special Agent Joseph G. Deegan, chief of extremist investigations at FBI headquarters, said at a special security conference in the Los Angeles FBI field office in 1977, after his testimony before the Church Committee: "We are the only ones who know what is good for the country, and we are the only ones who can do anything about it." The thought of becoming a whistle-blower was against everything I had ever believed in. It was the hardest decision of my life. I reviewed in my mind what I thought might be the reactions of nearly every friend I ever had, from childhood to my retirement. What would they think? What would they say? The answers were always the same. What was most important to me was what I thought of myself. If I were ever to have any self-respect, I had to square my experience in the FBI with my conscience and my country. Eighteen years after my retirement I still ponder my decision to become a whistle-blower.

This book is my legacy to the freedom-loving people of America who do not intend to forget what the FBI and the federal government did in the 1950s through the 1970s to suppress our freedoms guaranteed under the Bill of Rights. I am sure that American philosopher George Santayana, who lived from 1863 to 1952, was correct when he said, *"Those who forget the past are condemned to repeat it."* I have used pseudonyms to protect the privacy of some individuals and of some living agents who committed illegal acts, or who said or did anything grossly offensive. Each pseudonym is introduced in italics. The names of public figures and celebrities have not been changed. The names of places, FBI field offices, or FBI squads have not been changed.

Chapter 1

A Conventional Beginning

For an agent who became an unconventional whistle-blower, I had a conventional beginning, growing up in Steubenville, Ohio in the late 1930s and early 1940s as the straitlaced son of a junior high school principal who never drank liquor or swore. Dad used expressions like "Billy Blue Blazes," "Gee Whiz," "Ah, Horse Feathers," and "Oh, Shaw." Not once did I hear my dad say, "Damn," "Fuck," or "Shit." None of those four-letter words were in my family's vocabulary.

My mother considered herself refined. She helped found the local chapter of the Daughters of the American Revolution. The most disgusting word my mother, Ina, ever used was "nigger." She did not like "niggers," Jews, or foreigners in any way, shape, or form, and she let the family know it. I remember, as a boy, my mother making a fuss over world-renowned U.S. contralto Marion Anderson wanting to sing in Constitution Hall. The Daughters of the American Revolution refused to let Marion Anderson perform in Constitution Hall solely because she was black. Even Mrs. Eleanor Roosevelt could not persuade the Daughters of the American Revolution to acquiesce in their racism and bigotry.

When I was a child in the late 1930s, Dad and I listened to the cops-and-robbers radio program "Gangbusters" on our Philco radio on Sunday evenings. During the early years of World War II we had a close-up view of gangbusters. My mother rented rooms to FBI agents who were on the road. As we sat around the fireplace on cold winter nights, these agents told tales of how the FBI swooped down and arrested bank robbers. It was "Gangbusters" come to life.

I admired Mr. John Edgar Hoover, who directed the FBI from 1924 to 1972. I thought he knew what he was talking about. I was bubbling over with patriotism from my Navy service in 1945 and 1946. I was sure General George Patton was right when he declared that we should have taken the war to Russian soil and stamped out those "no good commie bastards." So no one in the family seemed surprised when I decided to join the FBI after having graduated from Ohio State University in 1950 with a degree in business administration.

Joining the FBI was initially my mother's idea. One of her former FBI agent tenants had written her that the FBI was recruiting special agents to handle the investigations of persons applying for jobs with the Tennessee Valley Authority. Congress had given the FBI the responsibility of investigating applicants for jobs regulated by the Atomic Energy Act. He wrote that Mr. Hoover had changed the educational requirements for Special Agents from a law or accounting degree to a degree from an accredited college.

Although I had a job with Kaiser Steel in Fontana, California, working at the iron ore mine at Desert Center near Palm Springs, Mom thought the job was beneath any son of hers who had a bachelor's degree. It did not matter to her that I wanted to go to Alaska for an adventure and to earn a stake to invest in California real estate. So, being a dutiful and obedient son and a solid patriot, I submitted an application to the FBI.

Just weeks after I applied to the FBI, Mother heard from her friends in the Daughters of the American Revolution and the Eastern Star, a Christian organization that is the women's equivalent of the Freemasons, that the FBI was investigating our family. Dad, who was a member of the widely distributed secret order of Free and Accepted Masons, had also heard from friends in Ohio that the FBI was investigating him and his family.

My dad told me that J. Edgar Hoover was a Mason. Mom told me that Hoover was one of the Daughters of the American Revolution's favorite lecturers on the invasion of America by foreign communists. I felt good about my chances of becoming an agent.

So while FBI agents were conducting a full-field investigation into every aspect of my background, education, character, loyalty, and associates, I prepared myself for the nine weeks of training I would have to undergo if accepted into the FBI. I ran a hard two miles in the open desert every day after work at an elevation of about 2,000 feet.

Then I pumped iron until dinner time. I could bench press my own weight eight times. At age twenty-four, I was in splendid physical condition and ready for Mr. Hoover's boot camp.

In May 1951, Mr. Hoover sent a letter directing me to report to room 633 in the Old Post Office Building in Washington, D.C.

When I entered the appointed room and looked around, I thought I had mistakenly come across a class of over-the-hill postal bureaucrats. All were older than I, some by as much as ten years. They were fat bald men, some with a bit of gray hair, and nearly all of them hopelessly out of shape. I quietly stepped back into the hall and closed the door. I looked again at Hoover's letter to make sure I was in the right place. I knew Mr. Hoover never made a mistake. I was in the right place. I returned and took a seat near the back of the room.

Donald Bird (not his real name), a man with dark features, short black hair, and a five o'clock shadow, stood behind the lectern. He introduced himself as the class counselor of New Agents Class #31.

A few minutes later, in stepped Assistant Director Hugh Clegg, a large strapping man who was overweight, out of condition, and out of breath. Clegg was the number three man in the FBI and head of the Training and Inspection Division. I learned later that his nickname was "Troutmouth."

Mr. Clegg barked, "Good morning, gentlemen," as he stepped behind the lectern. "Please stand, raise your right hand, and repeat after me: I, your name, do solemnly swear..." I glanced around the room at the men. We were all white Anglo-Saxons. Except for the difference in ages and body sizes we looked as if we had come from one mold.

I thought of my friends from high school, who were Negro, Jewish, Italian, and Mexican, who were killed in World War II or who had fathers and older brothers killed in action. They were not represented in the New Agents class. Also, there was not one female. I learned a few weeks later that Mr. Hoover did not tolerate women, Negroes, or minorities as Special Agents. At the time, I felt as though I was entering a private secret society. The same feeling had come over me when I had been in high school and had joined the secret society of the DeMolay, known within the society as the junior Masons.

"...so help me God."

We completed the oath. Overwhelmed, a tear rolled down my cheek. Mr. Clegg cleared his throat. He said, in a booming voice that needed no electronic assistance, "Congratulations, men. You are now Special Agents of the Federal Bureau of Investigation. Always remember, you are a personal representative of Mr. Hoover. Please, for your own sake, try not to embarrass the bureau."

Chapter 2

The Making of an Agent

Fifty men stood proudly with me as Hugh Clegg swore us into office. Only thirty-six were there nine weeks later, after our training period at the FBI's National Academy in Quantico, Virginia, when Clegg handed us our credentials and the coveted gold badge. Those nine weeks were a grueling and surprising introduction to the FBI.

Immediately after the swearing-in ceremony, our class counselor began to describe what Clegg meant about being Hoover's "personal representative." Bird said, in a Southern drawl, "Y'all will always present the appearance of a successful businessman. Mr. Hoover expects each of his Special Agents to wear a dark business suit, a white shirt, a dark conservative tie, dark socks, and black shoes. Argyle socks and colored socks are strictly forbidden."

We were to hear about Hoover's dress code hundreds of times over the years, but as Bird explained it for the first time, I carefully wrote down every point. Other new agents were also scribbling notes. Every item seemed terribly important. Bird said, "Your notebooks will be graded on neatness and thoroughness at the end of the course. They may be inspected anytime during training. The inspectors have a propensity for examining notebooks and personal belongings at Quantico while you are on the firearms range all day. If any of y'all have risqué photographs of girl friends or wives in your wallets I suggest you hide them properly."

"Don't exhibit any photographs in the lockers at Quantico. Mr. Sloan, the Special Agent in Charge of Quantico, does not want to open your locker to visitors and dignitaries and find pictures plastered on the doors."

"Remember, always wear a snap-brim hat whenever outdoors. Anybody who doesn't have a hat had best go out and buy one at lunchtime today. Don't wait until tomorrow or next week. Mr. Hoover or Inspector *Mudd* had better not catch any of y'all coming in and out of this building without a hat on your head."

Several other agents and I bought hats at lunchtime.

Bird and the other FBI officials who paraded in and out of the classroom over the next few weeks aimed hundreds of regulations at us. We were to walk up and down the staircase to our sixth floor classroom in the Old Post Office Building. One official explained, "Mr. Hoover does not want you to use the elevators because they are for the personnel of the Washington Field Office." The official told us about a clerk who had been fired for using Hoover's personal elevator in the Department of Justice building.

We were not to prop our feet against the wall during breaks between classes. We had to trim our hair regularly, at least once every other week. Instructors from the Training and Inspection Division often pointed out an agent in the morning class and told him that if he did not get his hair cut at lunchtime, he need not return to class.

Inspector William Mudd from the Training and Inspection Division delighted in demanding answers to obscure, nit-picky questions. For example, he would ask for the classification numbers of obscure statutes that had not been discussed in class, nor would be discussed for several days. He did not confine himself to the "Agent's Handbook," expecting us to know the specifics of every story printed in the newspaper.

I started to bury myself in the *Washington Post* at breakfast along with several other new agents, in an effort to be prepared to answer questions about details in world events. It did not make any difference. That day Mudd pointed to another victim and asked about an obscure item on the eleven o'clock TV news. I added watching the late news to my daily routine.

Not all new agents were intimidated by Mudd and the FBI's myriad of rules. During the third week, Mudd was in the middle of reading a section of the "Manual of Rules and Regulations" on how to fill out a travel voucher. *Joe Rio* stood up and said, "This is fucking bullshit, man." Rio then walked toward Mudd and threw down his handbook, pencils, and notebook. "And you can tell that fucking queer Jack Hoover I said so, asshole." Joe Rio walked out of the room, never to return.

Everyone was shocked, except for William Mudd. He just stood there and grinned. After a few moments, Mudd said, "That wasn't very smart. The Director won't be happy to hear what Mr. Rio thinks of the FBI training program. I certainly would not want to be Joe Rio looking for a job with a 'dismissed with prejudice' referral from J. Edgar Hoover."

I began to think that any minute the Mad Hatter would walk into the room and begin a lecture on bureau policy. But no matter how ridiculous New Agents class seemed, I could not bring myself to get up and leave. I had invested too much time and money to simply walk away. At the same time, I felt that William Mudd and some of the other instructors acted like children, and that their petty rules and regulations were stupid, at best.

If I thought that Mudd was the dumbest person I had ever met, it was only because I had not yet encountered Hank Sloan, the Special Agent in Charge of the FBI National Academy at Quantico, Virginia.

When we first arrived at the academy, Hank Sloan met our bus much the same way a schoolmarm greets a bus load of first-graders. Mr. Sloan directed us to a classroom where he explained *his* rules of Quantico. "There will be no whistling at any time while you are at Quantico, gentlemen," said the tall, thin, gray-haired Sloan in a thick Texas accent. "And y'all will not flush the toilet at the end of the building after 10 P.M.," pointing toward the dining room. "That's where my office and private quarters are located. If you have to use the head after 10 P.M., there are facilities at the other end of the building. No agent is to shower at either end of the building after 10 P.M."

A few of the agents snickered, not knowing whether or not Sloan was serious. From his expression after the snickers, it was clear he was deadly serious. Hank Sloan looked at those who had snickered and he jotted some notes. Mr. Sloan slept in his office at Quantico instead of going home, as the other Agents in Charge in the field offices did.

Sloan continued. "The most important thing to remember is how to make your bed." Sloan looked up from his notes to glance at the new agents and then looked down again. "Pillows are to be placed so that the open end faces away from the doorway. Your blanket must come down even with the bed frame."

Hank Sloan went on for another half hour giving us a precise description of how our beds were to be made every morning. He included details of exactly how many inches to fold down the sheet over the blanket. Sloan gave instructions on how to dust the floor and clean the windows and insisted that each room be immaculate. Then, Sloan said, menacingly, "If you do not do this correctly, gentlemen, you will answer to me. I will conduct a bed check at 9 every single morning you are here at Quantico. No agent is to be on the dormitory floors during classroom hours from 9 to 5:50, unless he is on official sick leave, approved by me."

This was worse than the Navy, I thought.

Mudd explained, "FBI agents are on duty twenty-four hours a day. Mr. Hoover must be able to reach you within the hour no matter where you are, no matter what you are doing."

Mudd laid out the procedure we had to follow while in Washington, D.C. (We alternated training between Quantico and Washington. The time at Quantico was used for intensive firearms training; time in Washington was used for technical training, defensive tactics, lectures on communism, administrative procedures, report writing, and moot court.) While training in Washington, we were to call the Washington field office every hour during the evening if we were away from our residence.

While the inspectors swiftly fired agents who broke any minor rule or regulation, they encouraged us to cheat to pass the training exams we were given. The passing grade on any exam or spot quiz was 85%. Before giving the first written quiz, Bird directed us to print our answers lightly in pencil. All questions were phrased to induce either a "yes" or "no," or "true" or "false" answer. An agent in a class ahead of us told me to print in capital letters. It was easy to erase a wrong answer and print the correct answer in capital letters.

Bird gave the answer to the first question, then he slowly read the question and repeated the answer. In this way, Bird and the other instructors, including Mudd, gave us time to change our incorrect answers. After finishing the quiz in silence, students would grade each other's papers. We were careful not to attract attention by making a perfect score of 100%. Everyone in class always made the magical grade of 85%.

As I watched my friend *Phil Starr* casually correcting my tests to make the magic 85%, I changed his papers for a passing grade. Although I was willing to put up with petty rules, cheating was not what I expected from the world-renowned FBI. I decided that if this was what the great J. Edgar Hoover and his mystical FBI represented, then that was what they were going to get. *Bullshit.*

I felt that I wanted to tell someone, but I knew no one would believe me if I said that FBI agents cheat on written examinations. My mother and father certainly would not have believed it about Hoover's FBI. I knew that if I had reported the cheating to the *Washington Post*, I would have been made a laughing stock. The FBI would have said I was a disgruntled employee who could not survive the FBI's intensive training. I was determined to take what the FBI dished out just to graduate from training school.

The only time an agent in our class flunked an exam was when Hoover's courtiers decided, for seemingly random reasons, that they did not like someone.

One day Mudd came to class with a three-question essay exam. When the test was over we did not exchange papers as with earlier tests. Mudd personally collected the papers and left the room. During the recess we all discussed the exam and agreed that most of us had missed one question, which meant an automatic score of 66%, low enough to be fired. I knew I missed one question. I thought surely I would be fired.

The next day Mudd marched into the classroom with the smugness of a prima donna. He singled out *John Mulrooney* and said he had flunked the test.

Mulrooney demanded to see the test scores. Mudd said, "Mr. Hoover has declared the tests Top Secret and Confidential. You are dismissed, Mr. Mulrooney."

Mulrooney threw his notebook and other bureau property on the floor. He left the room without even taking his straw hat that he had had to buy to attend class. Mudd left the room without further comment. Bird stood up and sheepishly said, "Men, let's take a fifteen minute break."*

Mulrooney was not the only one who disappeared suddenly. Early one morning an instructor from the Training and Inspection Division opened the classroom door and asked *Donald Lane* to step outside. Lane did not return, not even to hand in his handbook, notebook, or his pencils.

Once, I was questioned in an attempt to weed out undesirable agents. One afternoon, Sloan walked into the classroom and interrupted the lecturer to read six agents' names, including mine. We were to be driven to Washington for a personal interview with Clegg and Inspector Ken McIntire.

My heart flip-flopped. I felt sick. I felt certain that I was about to be fired.

The six of us rode in two cars, one driven by Bird and the other by *Stan Ray,* another New Agents class counselor. The ride to Washington was the worst hour I had ever spent in my life. Two of the six sat on either side of me in class. *Ted Swan,* who sat on my left, was my roommate in Washington. He had been a bank teller before joining the FBI and he was easily fifty pounds overweight. *Rod Swimmer,* who sat on my right, was average in height and weight. The fact is that he was so average that he was *nondescript.* They did not appear to fit my impression of the FBI mold, but then, what about me? Was I a misfit?

The interview with Inspector McIntire lasted only a few minutes. He asked some routine questions, such as where I had gone to college and whether I was married. He already knew the answers from my personnel file. He was more interested in my roommate Ted Swan, who was also being questioned.

---

* A month later when I was in Memphis, my first office, Bird told me in strict confidence that John Mulrooney had been fired because the Training and Inspection Division thought he was "too friendly." Bird said that the FBI had no evidence that Mulrooney was "queer," but that Mudd did not want to take the chance that Mulrooney might be hiding in the closet.

McIntire asked, "How long have you known Mr. Ted Swan?"

"I met him the first day of training school, sir."

"Aren't you two roommates when you're in Washington?"

"Yes, that's because we sit next to each other in class. Mr. Bird suggested we 'team up' during training to..." McIntire cut me off.

"What kind of guy is he?"

"He's the kind of man Mr. Hoover hires as an FBI agent, sir. He's soft and pudgy, a sissy, if you ask me. Not someone I'd like to have along on an arrest in a dark alley." I thought I was about to be fired, so I did not give a damn about playing psychological games with the FBI's Training and Inspection Division. "But if that's what Mr. Hoover wants working for him, it's fine with me, sir."

"I see," said McIntire, leaning back in his brown leather executive chair as he took a drag on the cigarette that had been smoldering in a brown glass ashtray the size of a dinner plate. McIntire concluded the interview after a few more questions about other classmates.

The following week all five of the agents who had made the trip to Washington with me were terminated. The class had been returned to Washington for a few days for the special firing of the five agents. That night I went to dinner alone at a restaurant near the rooming house where Swan and I had shared a room while in Washington. The waitress asked me where my "friend" was. I said, "My friend?"

She said, "The man you come in here with all the time — Isn't he your lover?"

The woman's comment shocked me to the core. I was never told by anyone why the five agents had been fired. I began to think that Mudd had thought they were homosexual. I expected the ax any day.

The following week we returned to Quantico. Hugh Clegg came to Quantico and interviewed everyone in class, except me. Clegg interviewed some agents two and three times. I asked one of the new agents, who had been a clerk for several years, why there were so many interviews and firings when the applicants had survived the background investigation. I was told that the inspectors feared for their jobs because if one "bad apple" becomes an agent it reflects upon the instructors, and Hoover would retaliate by transferring and demoting the instructors. I did not like the pressure. I was almost of a mind to tell Bird to fire me and get it over with.

For some reason, they did not fire me and I made it to the last and most important of tests—the final examination of the ninth week. It was not a written or oral examination where the passing grade was 85%. It was the test by the *man* himself, FBI Director J. Edgar Hoover. The director had not appeared before the class during the nine weeks of training. For this exam, we had to prepare for an audience with a man more powerful than the president. One's personal appearance on this day foretold an agent's future.

On the day of the exam, we lined up single file outside the director's office. A nervous inspector who looked like a funeral director opened the door. The class of thirty-six men, dressed in our finest dark suits, white shirts, and subdued neckties, black shoes, and black socks, passed in review of the director, shaking hands nervously and saying, "Hello, Mr. Hoover, my name is ——." We were like robots on an assembly line. All thirty-six of us were in and out of view of Hoover's piercing eyes within three minutes flat.

I had heard that an agent in an earlier class had said to the Director, "Hello, Mr. Jones, my name is Edgar Hoover." That agent was fired forthwith.

We returned to the classroom and talked about having met "The Man." Bird smiled, relieved that Hoover's inspection was over. Bird thought we all had passed inspection. Just then a gaunt gray-haired inspector from the Training and Inspection Division entered the room and shouted above the noise, "Mr. Hoover told [Associate Director] Mr. [Clyde] Tolson that this class has a pinhead and a truck driver." Before anyone could ask what he meant, the inspector turned and walked out of the room.

We looked at each other to see who had a pinhead. I saw one agent who could pass for a truck driver. He was big and burly and had a five o'clock shadow. I was not worried about being a pinhead, because my hat size is 7 1/4. But I was a member of the International Brotherhood of Teamsters, Chauffeurs, Warehousemen and Helpers, as a result of a former job—that made me a truck driver. I was worried.

Two agents did not show up the next day. One had a small head about the size of Mudd's head and the other had a five o'clock shadow much like Bird's. The big burly agent who I thought looked like a truck driver and who also had a five o'clock shadow was graduated, and he remained in the FBI until retirement.

Hoover had observed two "pinheads" in the previous class. The inspectors were afraid to ask Hoover or Tolson who the two agents were, so they checked the hat size of each agent and fired the two with the smallest hats. A fellow agent, who wore size 6 7/8 and who overheard the story, changed the tag inside his hat to read 7 1/2.

The swift and seemingly random nature of the firings created an atmosphere of precariousness and paranoia. I was relieved when, the day after the last two agents had been fired for being a pinhead and a truck driver, Bird passed out our letters of transfer. Bird handed me my letter and said, "Welcome to Memphis, Wes." Bird was also assigned to Memphis. I would have at least one friend in my first office.

Before leaving Washington, I asked Bird if the agents in the field were as uptight and jittery as the men in the Training and Inspection Division. Bird said that the mood of field agents is in direct proportion to the distance from Washington. I knew I could not take much more of stupid assheads like Mudd and Sloan. Bird's comment gave me hope that life would return to normal once I arrived in Memphis, Tennessee.

On my way to Memphis, I stopped in Saint Clairsville, Ohio, just long enough to get married to my fiancée, *Anne Dale*, who was the office secretary at the Calvary Presbyterian Church in Riverside, California. My parents and I were members of the church and they had arranged our meeting a year earlier. We spent the equivalent of a weekend honeymoon in the famous Peabody Hotel in Memphis.

I went to work the following Monday. The Special Agent in Charge,* Donald S. Hostetter, one of the FBI's best bank robbery

---

* In 1951, all FBI field offices were supervised by a Special Agent in Charge or SAC. All SACs had an Assistant Agent in Charge known as an ASAC. The smaller offices, like Memphis, did not have squads, so the

investigators, introduced me to the agent who would be my mentor, Ewell C. Richardson. As Special Agent in Charge of the San Diego FBI field office, Richardson had interviewed me for the FBI before I was accepted. I was surprised to see him working as a mere agent in Memphis. Richardson had no more authority in the Memphis field office than I did as a first office agent.

A few days before my interview with him, an ex-convict by the name of W.E. Cook, Jr. had killed a family of five in Oklahoma and dumped their bodies in a well. Cook had escaped into California and killed another person. Richardson was expected to capture Cook in California, but Cook escaped across the border into Mexico where he was arrested by Mexican police at Santa Rosalia, 600 miles south of the border.

Ewell Richardson had committed the ultimate sin—he had embarrassed the Bureau and Hoover by letting Cook escape into Mexico. Because Richardson was the last on a long list of special agents in charge to fail to stop Cook from travelling from Oklahoma to Mexico, Hoover demoted Richardson to a brick agent.

My first cases were job applicant matters related to the Atomic Energy Act's classification number 116. One case involved a black man who had applied for a custodial position with the Tennessee Valley Authority, a three-member board charged with developing the Tennessee River and its tributaries.

In 1951, the Memphis FBI office covered the northern half of Mississippi. I worked 116s on a road trip Monday through Friday. It was a learning experience because I did not know the social customs in the South, such as Negroes having to sit in the back of the bus, use their own rest rooms, and not eat where I ate. I also had to become used to the stifling heat and humidity of the Mississippi Delta.

The black man who had applied for the janitor's job with the Tennessee Valley Authority was from Belzoni, Mississippi. I ques-

---

field agents were divided into equal numbers and supervised by the ASAC and the SAC. The larger offices that did both criminal and security work had squads of twenty agents. These larger offices had squads that were supervised by supervisor agents who were under the watchful eyes of the ASAC and the SAC.

tioned a group of white men sitting outside a general store in Belzoni. I identified myself as a Special Agent with the FBI. I explained that I was conducting a background investigation on a Mr. *Elijah Smith,* who had applied for a job with the Tennessee Valley Authority.

The men shook their heads indicating they did not know a Mr. Elijah Smith. I said, "That's strange, because Mr. Smith is the son of Bessie and Jessie Smith and he has lived just down the road from here for twenty-one years."

A fat man sipped a glass of lemonade and then spoke for the others. "You talkin' 'bout that there nigger, Elijah Smith?"

"I am referring to a black man named Mr. Elijah Smith."

The fat man wiped his sweaty brow. "Sir, we don't refer to niggers as mister. I've know'd that there nigger Elijah since he was knee high to a grasshopper and he ain't no mister."

The fat man's racism incensed me.

Although I had never confronted my own mother's racism, the white fat slob in Belzoni was a different story. I did not have to tolerate him. I said, "I don't give a damn whether you like Negroes or not." I nudged the .38 Colt with my elbow. The fat man proceeded to answer all questions concerning Mr. Smith without further oratory about Negroes.

I related my experience to one of my supervisors back in Memphis, Cy Miller. He said, "Negro men are called niggers. We call Negro women niggress or niggra. Understood?"

In just a few short months of being in the FBI I had observed a dark side of cheating and bigotry that made me uncomfortable. Still, I did not want to quit a well-paying job that commanded worldwide respect. And I enjoyed some of the work, and believed it to be legitimate FBI activity.

After learning how to write 116 reports, I was assigned Selective Service Act cases known as 25s. My job was to locate men who were considered draft dodgers by the local Selective Service Board because the Board did not have an address where the registrant could be reached by mail. Nearly all the delinquents were young black men who had been lost in the paper shuffle because they could not read or write. The 25s had the elements of a good fugitive investigation without the risk of running into bad characters. I enjoyed the Selective Service cases and learned much about how to find individuals even when they are on the run from the law.

In my next case, I witnessed police brutality and a police cover-up, and had a hand in convicting the corrupt officers. The FBI had received a complaint that three black teenagers in Mississippi had been beaten by sheriff's deputies and that two of the teenagers had confessed to the murder of a white boy. The third black teenager had been so severely beaten that he had to be hospitalized.

The case was assigned to Donald Bird, my class counselor and a civil rights expert. Bird needed a witness and an observer. He selected me. I was honored.

We first interviewed the teenager in the hospital, who had been beaten so badly that he could not be jailed. He gave us a signed statement of how the sheriff's deputies had beaten him with wood paddles with holes in them, and with leather whips with long laces. We interviewed the other two teenagers in the sheriff's jail, and they gave us similar signed statements.

During our visit to the sheriff's office and jail, I saw the paddles and whips hanging on the wall as trophies. I remembered some Hollywood movies where I had seen fifteenth-century torture chambers. I thought the movies must have been made in this particular sheriff's office.

I was no stranger to these implements of terror. My father had used a wood paddle and a leather razor strap on me when he thought I had disobeyed his orders. It is no wonder the two boys confessed to murder. When my dad had whipped me, I would have confessed to being J. Edgar Hoover.

The shocking truth behind this case is that the white boy, who had wandered away from home for a few hours and was thought to have been murdered, was actually very much alive.

As a result of the FBI's intervention, the three black teenagers were released from the sheriff's custody.* The two sheriff's depu-

---

* Twenty-one years later I witnessed police racism and an innocent African American jailed for murder. This time it was not a fat southern sheriff wearing sunglasses, but the FBI and the Los Angeles Police

ties were tried in federal court and convicted of violating the three teenagers' civil rights. They were sentenced to serve six months in prison. I felt good about their conviction, although I had done nothing but watch Donald Bird do what he liked most: putting the bad guys in jail.

I felt better about Hoover's mandate against employing black special agents because I realized that Mr. Hoover's racism was not shared by all his employees. I saw, firsthand, that FBI agents defended innocent black people in a court of law. I was one of those agents, and I was proud to be an FBI agent.

One year after arriving in Memphis, Hoover transferred me to Chicago, Illinois. I was thrilled—my mind was full of images of gangsters, Tommy guns, and the FBI's famous machine gun battles of the 1930s. It was clear to me from Chicago's newspaper headlines that gangsters ruled a Chicago underworld element in the 1950s because gangland style murders averaged close to 100 a year in the Chicago area.

I was ready to show Mr. Hoover that I could handle the tough guys from Chicago. I learned how to disassemble and reassemble the Thompson submachine gun with my eyes closed. I thought someday I would meet up with gangsters like "Machine-Gun" Kelly, John Dillinger, "Pretty Boy" Floyd, and "Baby Face" Nelson.

But when I told my colleague and veteran agent *Vince Coll* of my big plans for Chicago, he said that Hoover did not recognize the existence of a mob in Chicago. According to Coll, Mafia leader Meyer Lansky's organization had enough on Hoover and Tolson, as closet homosexuals, that Hoover would never investigate the mob.

I laughed, thinking Coll was joking. I said he should be careful to whom he tells such stories. Coll insisted he was not joking. He made me promise never to tell anyone as long as he lived. I noted that it was true that FBI training school had taught nothing about organized crime.

The thought of Hoover and his associate Clyde Tolson being homosexual shocked me. There were jokes in training school about

Department who were the culprits. (See Chapter Nine).

Hoover and Tolson being homosexual, but I had passed off the jokes as being in bad taste. I did not like attacks on my idol, Mr. Hoover.

Rumors of Hoover's and Tolson's homosexuality continued to permeate the field offices for years, but no agent seemed to have any personal knowledge of an affair.

Still, Hoover did nothing about organized crime for thirty-seven years, until pressured to do so by Attorney General Bobby Kennedy in 1961. Ex-FBI agent Anthony Villano writes, "No president or lesser politician felt strong enough to confront Hoover and ask why he stubbornly refused to attack organized crime with the same zeal he had mounted against the 'public enemies' of bygone days and the Red Menace. [This oversight is] because the Bureau files held dossiers that detailed minor and major scandals and embarrassing moments that involved hundreds of elected officials and their families."

In fact, the Mafia held similarly damaging—downright explosive—files on Hoover. Today it's clear that Hoover disliked Bobby Kennedy and President John F. Kennedy because Hoover feared the Kennedys would prosecute Meyer Lansky as a gangster, and prompt Lansky to expose Hoover and Tolson as closet homosexuals.

Anthony Summers documents the basis for Hoover's fear in his 1993 book *Official and Confidential, the Secret Life of J. Edgar Hoover.* The book's dust cover states, "J. Edgar Hoover...was a closet homosexual and transvestite. Mafia bosses obtained information about Hoover's sex life and used it for decades to keep the FBI at bay. Without this, the Mafia as we know it might never have gained its hold in America."

Chapter 3

Chicago's 24-Men Burglary Squad

I had just turned twenty-five when I arrived in Chicago from Memphis on the Fourth of July weekend, 1952. I did not want to keep Mr. Hoover waiting for my services. Anne and I spent the weekend looking for an apartment. (The Chicago FBI office offered absolutely no help to agents arriving in the city.)

The day I reported for duty to the Chicago FBI field office, I was ready to take on the gangsters. I imagined car chases and gun battles, with mobsters in broadbrim hats driving black bulletproof limousines with balloon whitewall tires. I was ready to wipe out the mob—in the style of Eliot Ness and his Prohibition-era "Untouchables."

At the time, I thought the public allegations that Hoover's FBI refused to investigate the mobsters was just a clever ploy by Hoover to keep the gangsters off guard. I assumed the FBI must have had thick files on all Chicago mobsters.

After a short audience with the Special Agent in Charge and a quick tour of the office, I was assigned to the Communist Party underground surveillance squad. I knew something about the Communist Party from lectures in training school, but I knew nothing about surveillance. A few days later an agent from New York City, who did not know how to drive a car, was assigned to our surveillance squad. I knew my idol, Mr. Hoover, had a plan, so I did not question the wisdom of having agents on the surveillance squad who could not drive or who did not know the first thing about surveillance.

As a rookie, I realized it was too much to expect to be assigned gangster cases. I was excited to be assigned to the surveillance squad because it meant being outdoors, in the fresh air, away from the piercing eyes of the supervising agents, with no paper work to do except a surveillance log of the day's events.

I didn't even know how to use a car radio because the Memphis office had no radio station. I had used the telephone and the Western Union telegraph office to stay in touch with the office when I was in Mississippi. I had learned the radio jargon and "10" signals on the first shift. Each car had a list of "10" signals in the glove compartment.

The task of my surveillance squad was to follow Doris Fine and Lillian Green from 7:00 A.M. to 11:00 P.M., seven days a week. Doris Fine was the spouse of Fred Fine, a leader of the Communist Party in Illinois. Lillian Green was the spouse of Gil Green, another leader of the Communist Party in Illinois.

Fred Fine and Gil Green had been indicted by a federal grand jury for violation of the Smith Act of 1940. The FBI had obtained warrants for their arrest, and both men had fled Chicago.

By 1938, the newly formed House Special Committee on Un-American Activities (HUAC), also known as the Dies Committee, named after its chairman, Martin Dies, Democrat of Texas, had started to hurl charges of communism toward groups it did not like. The National Lawyers Guild (a national bar association for liberal attorneys who opposed the conservative and racially exclusive American Bar Association) was one target. In response, Congress passed the Alien Registration Act, a sedition act that became known as the Smith Act of 1940.

We were told to stay with Doris and Lil. As one might guess, we had days when we looked like the "Keystone Kops." For fun, Doris and Lillian drove slowly until they recognized our cars following them. At railroad crossings, they waited for an approaching train and crossed at the last second just before the gates dropped. They did it jokingly, when all they were about to do was to go to the grocery store in the next block. Doris and Lillian must have enjoyed the attention of the many young, thin, handsome FBI agents who followed them everywhere except into the ladies room. One of their pastimes was sun bathing in the park while agents ogled their tanned bodies. Although I liked watching the women in bathing suits, I felt as though I was a paid voyeur. I did not think that watching women sunbathe had anything to do with catching a communist fugitive.

Their apartments were bugged and their telephones were tapped. One day a recording was made of their telephone conversation about a new arrival on the surveillance squad. Doris asked Lillian if she had seen the gorgeous new surveillance agent with the golden hair and tanned body.

One fall day in 1952 the bug in Lillian Green's apartment went dead. *Charles Gray,* a sound technician and break-in expert, had to repair the unit. Gray asked me to join him. While the surveillance team followed Lillian and Doris, Charles Gray and I entered Green's apartment with a front door key. The surge of adrenaline I felt at surreptitiously entering Green's apartment gave me an unbelievable natural high. Gray could see that I was enjoying the thrill. He smiled and went about replacing the bug.

Although we had cheated on exams in training school, the instructors told us to follow the legal rules of evidence when conducting investigations. We were told that the U.S. attorney general authorizes all wiretaps. I understood that the wiretap on Lillian Green was legal in that it had been authorized by the attorney general, so our entry into her apartment to fix the broken unit was therefore legal.

Two months later, Gray asked me if I would like to do a black bag job. I had not heard the term before, because it had not been discussed in training school. Gray explained that it was an entry into a residence or office to conduct a search of someone's papers and personal effects.

Gray explained that the term "black bag job" came from the black leather doctor's bag in which agents carried burglary tools during the years of World War II, when Hoover first had authorized break-ins against American citizens. The term soon became an anachronism. I was ecstatic to have been asked, because it meant that I had been accepted by J. Edgar Hoover, the FBI, and the Chicago office as one of the most trusted agents in the bureau. The thought of doing a bag job was more exciting to me than going after mobsters. (See Appendix A for the logistics of a bag job.)

Gray said that if we were caught it would be our ass. I thought he meant that we would be in trouble for embarrassing Hoover the way Special Agent in Charge Ewell Richardson had embarrassed Hoover when Cook had escaped into Mexico. Since the attorney general authorized wiretaps and bugs, and we were not supposed to get caught, I thought the attorney general had authorized surreptitious entries.

The fact is that the FBI was asking me to violate the Constitution of the United States in order to, paradoxically, protect the Constitution from the alien traditions we in the FBI defined as "un-American," "subversive," and "communistic." I was not sure what this rationale meant, but it sounded good to me. At the age of twenty-five I was all for my country, right or wrong.

I understood this rationale to be the same as that used during World War II when the United States had authorized and ordered its soldiers to kill the enemy, which I had been prepared to do when I was in the U.S. Navy at that time.

On my first bag job, we broke into Fritzie Englestein's apartment. We were looking for evidence that would lead us to her husband David Englestein's whereabouts in the Communist Party underground. I followed Gray's every move. My heart raced 180 beats per minute. When I got home that evening I had a couple of extra martinis, but I did not tell Anne that I had just violated the Constitution and had broken state and local burglary laws. I felt badly, just as I would have had I murdered an enemy soldier by slitting his throat in hand-to-hand combat. The irony is that acts considered criminal at home are admired and decorated for in war. Anne knew I was following the families of communist fugitives, but that was it. Mr. Hoover forbade us to discuss our work with our spouses, friends, or family. Anne had no idea what I did all hours of the day and night.

Gray and I went on to regularly enter Englestein's apartment illegally, but we never found so much as a telephone number or an address for David Englestein. Fritzie was either well trained or she had no idea of her spouse's whereabouts.

The Communist Party had such a closely guarded underground network that the FBI had difficulty finding anyone. Major field offices across the country had installed illegal bugs and wiretaps in the homes of those in the underground. Several FBI field offices formed bag job squads, as did Chicago.

The bag jobs on Communist Party treasurer Leon Katzen during 1952 to 1954, however, were so successful that the FBI stepped up its bag job operations.

The other surveillance agents and I were taken from the surveillance of Doris Fine and Lillian Green on the days we bagged Leon Katzen. Two other agents, *Bill Vail* and *Tony Mann*, broke into Katzen's apartment while we kept a tight surveillance on him. Katzen was an extremely sensitive target because his financial records revealed the complete picture of the finances of the Communist Party of Illinois.

The bag jobs on Katzen began under the administration of John F. Malone, Special Agent in Charge of the Chicago FBI office. On March 26, 1953, a memorandum classified Top Secret was sent by Joseph P. McMahan, Security Coordinator of the Chicago office, to J. Edgar Hoover, under the initials of the new Special Agent in Charge, Kline Weatherford. The memo explained the success of the bag jobs on Leon Katzen "for the past six months." McMahan recommended Bill Vail and Tony Mann for cash awards. The physical surveillance agents, including me, were recommended for letters of commendation. Instead of cash awards, Vail and Mann received grade raises from Hoover. Hoover promoted them from GS-12 to GS-13 with a $1,000 raise each.

Vail and Mann's promotion to a higher annual salary was unusual because our squad did hundreds of bag jobs and received only letters of commendation or cash awards. A grade raise is permanent and lasts throughout one's career and into retirement with higher benefits.

A total of forty-two individuals knew of the illegal break-ins against Leon Katzen (see Appendix B for a partial listing). The bag jobs on Katzen were so productive that the Chicago office discontinued the surveillances on Doris Fine and Lillian Green in April 1953 and stepped up the number of illegal entries into homes and offices.

A week after President Eisenhower authorized heads of sensitive agencies, departments, and bureaus to summarily fire disloyal employees, I received my first assignment on a security case. I was to review the subject's FBI file, write an Investigative Summary Report, and place the subject on the FBI's secret arrest list known as the Security Index.*

I had never written a security report and I knew nothing about the procedure or the Security Index. My subject was Mollie West, Secretary of the Communist Party of Illinois, the second most important person in the Communist Party of Illinois. Her file was three volumes thick, with over 1,000 pages of Confidential and Top Secret documents. A report had never been written on Mollie West. I spent most of the next two weeks standing up and reading files atop the file cabinets, for there were not enough desks and chairs to go around the office.

I sat on an overturned wastebasket and used the corner of another agent's desk to do some of the rough drafting on the report. We had been told in training school that the FBI was the most efficient bureau in the federal government. I had studied Office Efficiency in college. If using wastebaskets for chairs and not having a desk to work at was the most efficient way of doing business, I wondered about the other government agencies that were supposed to be less efficient.

I recommended Mollie West for the Security Index with the special designation of DETCOM, which stood for "detain as a communist." This meant that in the event Eisenhower declared a national emergency, Mollie West was to be arrested and detained for being a communist. I also gave her the designation of a Key Figure as a result of her position as secretary of the Communist Party of Illinois. (I followed the Manual of Instructions to the letter because I knew that my idol, Mr. Hoover, knew best when it came to the threat of communists taking over the United States by force and violence. If Hoover had ordered me to, I would have gladly assassinated these no good commie bastards.)

---

* The Security Index was a secret FBI list of subversives who were to be arrested in the event of a national emergency. For many years not even the Attorney General knew of the Security Index.

The Chicago office had instituted a crash program to get all the known communists on the Security Index. Hoover wanted to be able to arrest as many individuals as possible in the event of a national emergency. We in the FBI fantasized about repeating Hoover's feat of arresting 10,000 individuals during the Palmer Raids of 1920.* We had compiled hundreds of names of financial contributors to the Communist Party from the bag jobs on Leon Katzen. We had also identified dozens of subversive contacts during the Fine and Green surveillances.

Although the Chicago office received newly assigned agents on a weekly basis, it was unable to keep up with 85% of its caseload of Communist Party members in Chicago. The office had thousands of cases on Communist Party members who had never been or never were investigated.

That June, Julius and Ethel Rosenberg, who had been convicted of giving atom bomb secrets to the Russians, were executed in the electric chair. When the word arrived in the Chicago office the next day, Saturday, the agents who were working overtime to keep up with the office average overtime and to get their reports in to the bureau, began to celebrate. Some agents quit work and headed for the local pubs to toast the Rosenbergs' execution. Although I hated what the Rosenbergs had done to our country, I did not feel I should celebrate their electrocution. I was then and am now haunted by the one question that Mr. Hoover had for Ethel Rosenberg in case she recanted at the last moment on death row. It was rumored that Ethel was to be asked at the last minute, "Did you know that your husband was a spy for the Russians?"

---

* Attorney General A. Mitchell Palmer and those of his ilk in the Department of Justice, including J. Edgar Hoover, who at that time was a Department of Justice employee, decided in 1919 that the best way to save the country from alien radicals was to deport all the foreigners. The mass raid deportation plan, which Hoover helped formulate, was put into effect in November 1919. In January 1920, federal agents arrested an estimated 10,000 suspected alien radicals without warrants. Mr. Palmer told the Senate Investigating Committee that J. Edgar Hoover had been in charge of the arrests. Hoover testified before the Senate and protected Palmer by blaming the bureau for the 10,000 illegal arrests.

That summer Anne and I bought a house in Park Forest, Illinois. Park Forest was a new development thirty miles south of Chicago serviced by the Illinois Central Railroad commuter train. The houses were all two bedroom, one bath, single family units on a concrete slab with forced air heating. They had 750 square feet and they sold for $11,995. With the GI Loan of 3%, the monthly payments including principal, interest, taxes, and insurance were $68. It was our first home.

The commute was fifty minutes during rush hour on the express train. If I had to do an early morning surveillance or bag job it meant getting up at 3:00 A.M. and catching the 3:30 A.M. local train out of Matteson. That put me in the office about 5:15 A.M. with a brisk walk across the loop.

The move to Park Forest was good for Anne. She had a degree in Education from Ohio State University. Although we had attended Ohio State University at the same time, we never met on campus because Anne attended the College of Education and I attended the College of Commerce. She took a job teaching grade school in Park Forest.

On June 26, 1954, I personally arrested Claude Mack Lightfoot, Chairman of the Communist Party of Illinois, for violation of the Smith Act of 1940. (See Appendix C for an account of the arrest.) This was the Chicago office's first arrest of a Communist Party activist—accomplished more through luck than good investigation. J. Edgar Hoover commended me for the arrest. By the middle of August 1954, 117 individuals had been arrested nationwide and eighty-one had been convicted for violation of the Smith Act of 1940.

The U.S. Supreme Court ruled in 1957 that the Smith Act was an unconstitutional infringement on the right of free speech.

After Lightfoot's arrest, Hoover ordered the Chicago office to form a burglary squad to intensify the campaign against the Communist Party. The burglary squad in Chicago, known as the Communist Party Infiltration Squad or Security Squad Number 1, was divided into two twelve-man operational units. Each agent had two or three subjects assigned to him. The purpose of the squad was to conduct a survey on each subject to determine the feasibility of a bag job. When a subject was ready for a bag job, the twelve-man unit worked on that one subject for the day. If a surveillance and a bag job had particular problems, then all twenty-four agents were used to assure adequate security.

We did bag jobs around the clock. When people were at work we bagged their homes. When they were home we bagged their offices. We became break-in fanatics.

There were times when I did two and three bag jobs in one day. I went into the apartment of Adolph Rabin, an underground courier whose case was assigned to me, more than a hundred times. On days when other agents did not have bag jobs going that needed assistance, I entered Rabin's apartment every time he left his building.

Our original goal was to neutralize the Communist Party. But we lost sight of our goal as we intensified the number of break-ins. We extended our targets beyond the Communist Party.

In December 1956, Hoover asked Attorney General Herbert Brownell for authority to wiretap the home of Elijah Muhammad of the Nation of Islam, on the grounds that members of the Nation of Islam disavow allegiance to the United States. Brownell approved the wiretap surveillance. To Hoover, this meant that he could also do bag jobs on the Nation of Islam, but the only plausible reason for the FBI to break into the homes of members of the Nation of Islam was Hoover's hatred for African Americans and Hoover's desire to keep Elijah Muhammad from becoming a messiah for African Americans. We bagged the residence of two Nation of Islam members and photographed membership lists and financial records, even though the Nation of Islam was not a threat to the U.S. government. I acted as the lookout for the bag jobs on members of the Nation of Islam while fellow agents broke into their homes.

The bag jobs on the members of the Nation of Islam came after I had spent five years on the Communist Party Infiltration Squad. By then the Supreme Court had ruled that the Smith Act was unconstitutional. We had no authority for the bag jobs we did, and so we in the FBI were the ones who violated the Constitution. When we started bag jobs on a black religious organization, I knew then that the FBI was out of control, but I could not stop it because no one would have believed me—not even Hoover's most severe critics. If I had said anything, Hoover would have had me prosecuted for violating local burglary laws.

Chapter 4

A Close Encounter

Chicago, Illinois, Fall 1954

As an undercover burglary squad member, I prided myself on passing for an ordinary laborer. The olive drab canvas bag that I carried blended with the image I tried to convey, that of a janitor or building superintendent. I wore a tan windbreaker frayed at the cuffs, a faded red plaid shirt, gray paint-stained trousers, and tan work boots. Many of us on the Infiltration Squad bought our clothes at the Sears, Roebuck and Company store because the head of security, an ex-FBI agent, had given us Sears employee discount cards.

My fellow surveillance agents called me Ivan. During Chicago's cold winters, I wore a heavy fur-lined coat with a high fur collar and a Trooper's fur hat with ear flaps that tied under the chin. I looked like the first czar of Russia, Ivan IV, also known as "Ivan the Terrible."

My partner, Charles Gray, could not give up the polished look of an FBI agent to go undercover. Still, Gray was one of the FBI's best-trained black bag job experts. He had developed his burglary expertise during World War II, fighting against the Chicago members of Fritz Kuhn's German-American Volksbund, a Nazi-inspired organization in the United States. Fritz Kuhn, born in Germany, had set himself up as the American Führer.

Hoover had authorized us to enter the apartment of *Earl Dunn,* who was a labor organizer for the Chicago-based United Electrical Workers Union and a member of the Communist Party of the United States. Mr. Hoover had ordered Gray and me to find evidence in Dunn's apartment that indicated the Communist Party was using Earl Dunn to dominate or influence the labor union. Hoover also wanted evidence of any criminal violations. Hoover would have even used traffic tickets or parking violations as counterintelligence to embarrass Earl Dunn, the United Electrical Workers Union, or the Communist Party.

Charlie and I had bagged Dunn many times, so the day when we almost got caught appeared to be routine.

Dunn lived in a four-story red brick walk-up, in a mixed neighborhood of Jews and African Americans, on Chicago's South Side just north of the University of Chicago. *Fred Barr,* our driver, had dropped us off around the corner from Dunn's apartment building. *Bill Rapp,* our lookout, was parked across the street in a 1953 light blue four-door Chevrolet sedan. We had nicknamed Bill Rapp "Friendly," because he always had a smile.

Gray and I attracted little attention as we entered the building. Within seconds we were at Dunn's apartment door on the third floor. Gray put a key in the lock, turned the knob, and stepped quietly inside. No one appeared to be home, but we had to be sure. I checked the kitchen and the bathroom while Charlie tiptoed into the bedroom. The wood floors creaked as we moved from room to room.

When I joined Charlie in the bedroom he was on his hands and knees peeking under the bed. I did not say anything. I just smiled. I zipped open the olive canvas bag containing the ten-pound Motorola walkie-talkie developed originally for the military in World War II. I adjusted the antenna, put in the ear plug, and held the microphone to my mouth and whispered, "Ivan to Friendly, the players are on the field."

Friendly answered, "Ten four, Ivan."

I heard Friendly pass the word to radio control, in our downtown loop office, that the game had started. I heard *Mary Belfast,* our radio operator, tell the other surveillance agents following Dunn that "The ball game is underway."

I picked up the brown camera case Charlie had put down by Dunn's desk in the living room. I put the camera case on a chair and opened it. Inside was a 35 millimeter Leica camera attached to the lid with powerful lights mounted on each side. It had been developed by special agents in the FBI's laboratory in Washington, D.C., just for this kind of Top Secret operation. All I had to do was plug the electric cord into a 110-volt outlet, place the documents inside the marked space in the briefcase under the camera, and snap the shutter. The shutter automatically cocked when I plugged in the electricity. Hoover's laboratory agents had thought of everything for this clandestine operation.

Charlie and I did not speak as we went about rifling the notes on Dunn's desk and in the drawers. We knew exactly what we were after: names, addresses, telephone numbers, financial records, anything that linked Dunn and the Communist Party with other political groups or with the United Electrical Workers Union.

Charlie handed me some typed documents. I photographed the documents and returned them to Charlie. I carefully sifted through a stack of papers in the desk drawer. I did not bother with the various political tracts and union leaflets, but I did make notes. Charlie handed me some notes in longhand, presumably in Dunn's handwriting. Just then I heard a muffled explosion outside and passed off the noise as a backfiring car and calmly went about my work.

Suddenly, Friendly shouted over the radio, "A man's been shot on the front steps! I'll pick you up in the alley!"

My stomach wrenched. I thought, "Was this the day we would be caught?" I ran to the window but could not see any activity on the street below. I told Charlie what had happened. Charlie bent over and grabbed his stomach. From his twisted expression I knew he was in pain.

I ran back to the desk, grabbed the electric cord, and slammed the camera case shut. With the briefcase and the radio in hand, I ran to the kitchen. As I looked out the rear window to see if the way was clear, I expected to hear police sirens any minute. I thought the neighbors would have come outside by now, but the neighborhood was quiet. I looked over my shoulder and saw Charlie walking slowly through the kitchen with his arms around his stomach.

"What's wrong?"

"It's my ulcer."

"Can you make it?"

"Go ahead, I'll make it, or Hoover will have my ass."

My heart pounded as I started down the iron fire escape. I could not remember feeling so vulnerable. What if someone looked out and saw us—two white guys carrying bags and running down the fire escape from a black man's apartment?

Once in the alley, we jumped into the waiting car. Friendly floored the throttle. The tires screeched all the way to 55th Place. There was no traffic on the street. Friendly turned east at 55th Place toward Lake Shore Drive and safety.

The twenty-four-men bag job squad in Chicago was not an anomaly. The number of FBI bag jobs, based upon my personal experience, was about 23,800 over thirty-five years. That is only 68 bag jobs a year for each of the ten offices engaged in regular break-ins.

The following names are those I remember of suspected Communist Party leaders in Chicago on whom we did bag jobs:

Emanuel Blum
Richard Criley
Lou Diskin
Earl Durham
Rose Durham
James Durkin
David Englestein
Fritzie Englestein
Doris Fine
Fred Fine
Mollie Gold
Sam Gold
Gil Green
Lillian Green
Charles Hall
Flo Hall
Yolanda Hall
Mary Hortotsos
Leon Katzen
Sam Kushner
Claude Lightfoot
Adolph Rabin
William Sennett

Ed Starr
Sylvia Starr
Ray Tillman
Alfred Wagenknecht
Otto Wangerin
Mollie West
James West

There are others I have forgotten, such as the members of the Nation of Islam—some fifty targets in all that fade into the menagerie of hundreds of illegal FBI operations.

There were other squads in the Chicago FBI office that conducted bag jobs on a regular basis. The late Forest "Frosty" Thompson worked on the Socialist Workers Party squad. He told me that he and other agents on the squad did a bag job on members of the Socialist Workers Party about once a week. *Anthony Rust* and *Ewell Borne*, who worked the Socialist Workers Party in Chicago in the early 1950s, once told me they had done nearly 100 bag jobs on the Socialist Workers Party.

Adolph Hutt, who went from the Security Division in Chicago to the Criminal Division to work the Top Hoodlum Program, told me that he and other agents had done hundreds of bag jobs on the Mafia. Hutt said the FBI had bugged two dozen mob families through illegal break-ins in the Chicago area.

The following are other organizations that were victims of FBI bag jobs in Chicago:

American Civil Liberties Union
Chicago Committee to Defend the Bill of Rights
Chicago Committee to Secure Justice for the Rosenbergs
Civil Rights Congress
Committee to Secure Justice for Morton Sobell
Communist Party Headquarters in Chicago
Fair Play for Cuba Committee
Midwest Committee for the Protection of the Foreign Born
Modern Book Store
National Association for the Advancement of Colored People
National Lawyers Guild

Nation of Islam
Nationalist Party of Puerto Rico
Progressive Labor Party
Veterans of the Abraham Lincoln Brigade

Up until 1955 I thought the bag jobs we did on the Communist Party and its members had the sanction of some higher authority other than J. Edgar Hoover. I expected the Attorney General to have authorized break-ins as he had done with wiretaps. It was not until the new Assistant Special Agent in Charge of the Chicago office, Joseph L. Schmit, explained in very clear terms that black bag jobs were completely illegal that I realized the full impact of what the other agents and I had done. I understood for the first time that Hoover and the FBI could disown us if we were caught.

Mr. Schmit said that if we were ever caught we would be dismissed with prejudice—the most severe comment Hoover could make against a fired employee. By then I was so deeply involved in doing illegal searches and developing anonymous sources that the only way out was to go on and try not to be caught.

By 1956, I was assigned to the cases of many of what the FBI called "Key Figures" and "Top Functionaries" of the Communist Party in Chicago. Reports had to be submitted to FBI headquarters every three months. Part of the work required the reading of Communist Party literature and the speeches of the leaders. I frequently found information in these reports indicating that a person had opposed the Broyles Bill in 1951, which was enough to make them subversive even if they were not Conmmunist Party members.

In 1951, the Illinois State Legislature had held hearings at Springfield, Illinois concerning Senate Bill 102, commonly referred to as the Broyles Bill. It had been sponsored by State Senator Paul V. Broyles for the general purpose of confining and restricting the activities of the Communist Party and other subversive groups in the State of Illinois. It would have required school teachers and others to sign a loyalty oath. The Broyles Bill did not pass, but in Hoover's mind, opposing its passage was as good as breaking a law.

I questioned the ethics of the Broyles Bill. It struck home because state employees would be asked to swear loyalty to the leaders of the state. I was troubled because I realized that I too could be required to sign a loyalty oath. Swearing to protect and defend the Constitution is one thing. Swearing to protect a leader who tramples on the Constitution is quite another matter.

I was protecting Hoover and the FBI by not exposing the illegal bag jobs. I did not like the idea but I did not want to blow the whistle on such a powerful leader as J. Edgar Hoover, who would have had me for lunch. I secretly opposed signing a loyalty oath while all the time I wrote reports on suspected subversives who opposed the Broyles Bill.

Although black bag jobs were illegal—in violation of the U.S. Constitution and of state and local laws—J. Edgar Hoover, Clyde Tolson, and other top officials often rewarded special agents for developing especially productive anonymous sources.

The entire squad of twenty-four agents received cash awards of $150 each for a total single outlay of $3,600. (See Appendix D for Hoover's award to me.) In today's currency, that would be about $36,000 for developing "highly confidential sources of information," bureau-ese for black bag jobs.

Chapter 5

The Security Index

Hoover's Secret Arrest List

Nineteen fifty-six was a busy year both on and off duty. I bought a new Ford Thunderbird convertible through a Chicago office contact for $100 above the dealer's cost. The dealer personally delivered the red and white car to my front door in Park Forest. With that purchase, Anne had her own car to drive to work instead of using a car pool with other teachers. I drove the Mercury to the Illinois Central train station each workday.

A year earlier I had bought a Star class sailboat, an Olympic class racing yacht. It was twenty-two feet in length and was built about the time I was born. The Star is a one-design class, which means it does not change dimensions or style of rigging as do the boats that compete in the America's Cup race. The marinas in Chicago had long waiting lists for moorings. I had to keep the boat in Michigan City, Indiana, about a one-hour drive from Park Forest. Anne and I spent as many summer weekends as possible sailing around Michigan City. I became an avid sailor, but Anne did not like the boat nor did she like driving to and from Michigan City with the Thunderbird top down. I liked the convertible so much that on cool fall days when I drove alone I put the top down and turned on the heater to keep my legs warm.

During the winter months I did woodworking. I designed, built, and upholstered a seven-foot couch, a matching lounge chair, two barrel back chairs, a game table with an inlaid chess board, two single bed frames, and a display case for Anne's cut glass pieces. The display case was fastened to the wall. It had a fluorescent light in the base under a glass shelf. The entire case was covered with black felt. It was an interesting display at night and acted as a good back-light for watching television.

After five years in the FBI, four years of which involved my participation in violations against the Constitution and my surveillance of individuals who had a constitutional right to voice their opinions against the FBI and the government, I began to contemplate my future role in the FBI. I had not been chasing federal law violators as I had hoped. The fact is that I did not know of any Communist Party members who had violated any laws, except possibly parking and traffic laws. I had not joined the FBI to become a traffic cop. I wanted to catch bank robbers and car thieves. I asked for a transfer to a criminal squad but was refused.

Instead, I was assigned about two dozen cases of Key Figures and Top Functionaries of the Communist Party, including such leaders as Richard Criley, David Englestein, Yolanda Hall, Leon Katzen, Sam Kushner, Claude Lightfoot, Bill Sennett, Otto Wangerin, Alfred Wagenknecht, and Mollie West—apparently, my report writing ability on Mollie West in 1953 had not gone unnoticed. Reports had to be submitted every three months. No sooner had I finished with the last person on the list than I began the list over again for another ninety-day report. After the second round of ninety-day reports the paper work became boring. There was little choice—either I did it or I quit the FBI.

I became very knowledgeable about the Security Index, because all my subjects were on the Security Index and were tagged either DETCOM ("detain as communist") or COMSAB. COMSAB was the designation for someone who had a job in a company with government contracts, and who therefore had an opportunity to commit sabotage in the event of a national emergency. Subjects tagged COMSAB were to be arrested first, then those tagged DETCOM, followed by all the others on the Security Index.

After all the individuals on the Security Index were arrested, those on the Communist Index, later called the Reserve Index, were to be arrested.

The Communist Index, also a Top Secret index that neither the Attorney General nor the President knew about, consisted of those individuals whose subversive activities did not bring them within the Security Index criteria, but who, in a time of national emergency, were in a position to influence others against the national interest or were likely to furnish material financial aid to dangerous elements due to their subversive associations and ideology. Included were individuals falling within the following categories:

1. Professors, teachers, and educators.
2. Labor union organizers or leaders.
3. Writers, lecturers, newsmen, entertainers, and others in the mass media field.
4. Lawyers, doctors, and scientists.
5. Other potentially influential persons on a local or national level.
6. Individuals who could potentially furnish material financial aid.

The only differences between the Security Index and the Communist Index—beside the differing priority given each—were the file drawers in which the two different cards were placed and the distinctive color of the Communist Index cards. Security Index cards were white. The Communist Index cards varied in color depending upon whether a person was a school teacher, a labor union organizer, a writer, a doctor, a lawyer, a rich person, or a business leader.

Together, the Security Index and the Communist Index totaled approximately 50,000 names in Chicago. (This estimate is based on my observation of the number of cards per file drawer and the number of file drawers.) The Security Index consisted of approximately 5,000 names. The Communist Index, or Reserve Index, consisted of approximately 45,000 names. I estimated at one point in time in the mid-1950s that if there had been a national emergency it would have been necessary to set up tents in Soldier Field on Lake Shore Drive to house all those to be arrested.

Many of Hoover's categories for the Communist Index bothered me because I had friends and neighbors in Park Forest who were not the least bit subversive but who disliked anything resembling a loyalty oath like that of the proposed Broyles Bill. Anne was certainly a loyal American who opposed the idea of communism, but she also opposed the idea of having to sign a loyalty oath to some half-baked politician who had no ethics and who worked for the party contributor with the largest bank account. I knew no teachers in Park Forest who wanted to sign away their ethics to a political leader like Mayor Richard J. Daley, who controlled the politics and the city of Chicago in the 1950s.

If I had been a teacher or doctor or lawyer, I would have opposed pledging my loyalty to Mayor Daley. As an FBI agent I did not want to pledge my loyalty to any politician with Daley's reputation of strong-arm tactics.

At first, I liked adding names to the Security Index because I thought it would help if we had to arrest potential saboteurs in the event of war with Russia. As my knowledge of the Security Index grew, I saw that other agents and I were adding names to the list just to please Hoover and those of his ilk at the bureau. We created a list as large as that which Hoover had had when he was in the General Intelligence Division of the Department of Justice, with an index of 450,000 foreign radicals, organizations, and publications. The FBI's nationwide Security Index and Communist Index peaked at around 500,000 names. I did not like the seemingly senseless act of building such an arrest list just because Hoover suffered from xenophobia.

When I received a call one day from one of the criminal squads to join them on a surveillance, I thought that my prayers to join a criminal squad had been answered, but I soon learned the reason for the call. I had been in the FBI for five years and had not testified before a federal grand jury, and Hoover wanted his agents to have the experience of testifying in court.

Since I had worked bag jobs and underground surveillances in Chicago, I had had no chance to appear in court. The surveillance I joined was on a man from New York who was selling various forms of pornography in Chicago. After the suspect sold what merchandise he could, he headed back to New York. Just when he crossed the Illinois border into Indiana, establishing evidence of a federal violation to transport pornography interstate, agent *Gustov Puffnik* stopped the suspect's car and placed him under arrest while I acted as an observer. I assisted in counting the rolls of movie film and other items. The day I testified before a grand jury on this case, I noticed two rolls of film missing from the inventory. I asked Puffnik about the missing rolls of film. He said *Ronley Bonneville* had taken the two rolls of film for his personal collection at home.

I was furious that Bonneville had stolen government evidence before I had completed my testimony before the grand jury. Bonneville was the third most senior official in the Chicago FBI office, so I could not report him without my getting into trouble. This collector of pornography was later chosen as the Parent Teacher Association "Parent of the Year." Ronley Bonneville retired in 1970 with twenty-nine years in the FBI.

If the U.S. Attorney General had asked me how many rolls of film had been recovered from the suspect's car, I would have had to lie under oath to protect Bonneville and Puffnik, because I would not have been able to explain the two missing rolls of pornographic film.

Just as disgusting as the pornography case was the liquor hijacking case I helped with one night. My partner and I received a call, while working a communist surveillance, to look for a certain stolen tractor trailer truck loaded with liquor that might be in our area. We found the truck parked in a dark alley and kept it under observation until the criminal squad agents arrived on the scene. The FBI agents from the hijacking squad loaded up their bureau cars with cases of liquor before reporting the recovered amount to the insurance company, the bureau, and the court. I had witnessed the corruption, but I could not report it because I would have been disciplined for alleging that agents had taken recovered stolen property.

I was sick of working bag jobs, adding people to Hoover's secret arrest list, and learning of FBI agents stealing evidence. I wanted out of Chicago.

The time spent on the commuter train riding to and from work gave me about two hours a day to read, study the stock market, and learn Spanish. I studied the Standard and Poor's Investment Advisory Survey and made small stock investments according to their recommendations. I had made enough money in the market to buy the Ford Thunderbird with cash.

I taught myself Spanish through the use of the books and records of the Linguaphone Institute Limited, London, England. The many hours of studying Spanish while riding on the train and sitting on surveillances prepared me for the FBI's Spanish language test. Agent friends who had studied Spanish in high school and college were being transferred to places such as San Juan, Puerto Rico; El

Paso, Texas; Albuquerque, New Mexico; San Diego, California; and to the position of legal attaché in Madrid, Spain.

I took the FBI's Spanish language test and passed. This was to have given me an opening to attend the Spanish language school in Monterey, California. I had the same seniority as other agents in Chicago who had been transferred to Monterey. I fully expected to go to Monterey for the next class, or the one after that.

Cornel Rockne, who had worked the Nationalist Party of Puerto Rico, had received a transfer, at his request, to one of the criminal squads. Supervisor Joseph M. Culkin, with whom I had done hundreds of bag jobs, wanted me to take over all the individual subject cases, and three informant cases for the Chicago caseload of the Nationalist Party of Puerto Rico, because I could speak some Spanish. The Chicago office had replacements, but Culkin wanted me. I accepted the change in assignments, thinking I could improve my Spanish and at the same time learn about the Nationalist Party of Puerto Rico on the off chance that I might someday be transferred to San Juan, Puerto Rico, one of my three offices of preference.

I had not handled live informants before then. Dealing with real informants who spoke Spanish was a new experience. I soon discovered that only one informant in the Nationalist Party of Puerto Rico in Chicago was worth anything. Rockne had nursed two other informants just to maintain his image and to stay within the informant quota.

I could not tell Joe Culkin that Rockne had two bogus informants because Culkin would pass the buck and tell the Special Agent in Charge of the office, Richard D. Auerbach, and Rockne would be in trouble for falsifying government documents. I would then be in trouble for informing on a fellow agent. I did the only thing I could do. I wrote bogus informant reports for two of the informants based on information from the one good informant, just as Rockne had done. After a few months of writing fraudulent informant reports, I phased out one of the bogus informants, claiming that he was in bad health. Two months later I closed the other bogus informant, claiming a family hardship, because I did not want to continue Rockne's fraudulent informant program. When my number of informants dropped below the quota, Culkin arranged to have two other Spanish-speaking informants, from another organization, infiltrate the Nationalist Party of Puerto

Rico. Those two informants were then assigned to me. I soon discovered that one of those two informants was a fraud, and I discontinued that informant for lack of productivity.

Corruption permeated the Chicago office, so I was not surprised when I heard that agents had violated the kidnapping statute. In March 1957, FBI agents kidnapped *Kriskovivich Kirov*, a Soviet military intelligence major, who had visited Chicago on a spy mission. They transported him to Wisconsin, where he was held for over two weeks in a remote cabin. FBI agent *Kazan Saratov* told me later that he and agent *Bradford Leeds* had interrogated Kirov for eight hours a day, seven days a week, but Kirov had repeated only his name, rank, and serial number.

Saratov said that after a few days Kirov appeared to be disorientated, even though he had received regular meals and sleep. At the end of the first week Kirov could not remember his name and he confused his serial number. At the end of the second week Kriskovivich Kirov acted as though he had been given a lobotomy and appeared to be losing control of his bodily functions.

Saratov said he and Leeds became worried and so they called in a psychiatrist. Dr. *Snifildorf* examined Kirov for several hours. Saratov said that at the end of the examination the doctor turned to Saratov and said, "This man is so well trained that if you continue questioning him he will lose his mind completely. This man is worthless to you in his present state. I doubt whether he will ever be normal even if he makes it back to the Soviet Union."

I was aware that the spy world can be rough and that the Soviet Union's KGB was not a group of altar boys. But, the Soviet Union was considered to be an evil empire. I wondered how much less evil we were than they if we used tactics of the KGB. In the United States, kidnapping is kidnapping. The FBI had not had a court order or permission from the Attorney General to do what they had done to Kirov. I wondered just how far Hoover and his agents would go to protect what I began to see as their image of what was good for the country.

In 1958, Anne and I sold our house in Park Forest and bought a house in Dune Acres, an exclusive development on the shores of Lake Michigan near Chesterton, Indiana. We had discovered Dune

Acres during our sailing trips to Michigan City. Anne found a teaching job in Chesterton.

We enjoyed our free time in Dune Acres. During the summer we played on the beach. I sold the Star sailboat and bought a sixteen-foot wood lapstrake runabout with a thirty-five horse power Johnson Evenrude electric starter motor. We water-skied as often as possible. We kept the boat on the beach in the summer. It was a safe neighborhood, and our friends whose houses overlooked the boat on the beach could let us know of any trouble.

When I told Joe Culkin about my new house in Dune Acres he suggested I write a letter to Hoover explaining that I had just bought a home in Dune Acres and would not be available to attend language school in California. Culkin's suggestion seemed reasonable because I did not want to sell the house a few weeks after buying it and I thought that I could pick the time for my transfer to language school with Culkin's recommendation. If I could not control the timing of a transfer, at least I would be living in a nice area on the Lake Michigan shore. I believed this would ease my mixed emotions about the FBI. Culkin approved my letter to Hoover about being unavailable for language school.

While I enjoyed our new home in the isolation of Dune Acres with its pristine beach and clear water, the FBI's intimidation tactics and corruption continued to bother me. That year, Hoover had authorized the publication of a collection of works by FBI agents entitled *Masters of Deceit: The Story of Communism in America and How to Fight It.* (The publishers, Henry Holt and Company, falsely claimed the book was written by Hoover.) To ensure success of the book, Hoover issued a royal mandate that every special agent in the FBI buy at least one copy.

Agent *Bill McFrugal* of the Chicago field office refused to buy a copy of *Masters of Deceit,* because he thought it was a collection of the FBI's communist propaganda designed to scare the American public into believing Hoover knew best about communism. The Special Agent in Charge of Chicago transferred McFrugal to the applicant squad.

Sam Fudd, who worked bank robberies in Chicago and who worshipped Hoover, bought 100 copies of *Masters of Deceit* and gave the book as gifts to his wife, his wife's parents, his parents, his brothers and sisters, his wife's brothers and sisters, his aunts and uncles, his nieces and nephews, his neighbors in Park Forest, and his friends and neighbors back in Iowa. I asked Sam Fudd why he had bought so many books and he said he had a big family and could not afford to be transferred.

After looking at my copy of the book, I told Bill Rapp that Hoover was the real "Master of Deceit." With a poker face, Rapp asked if I was a pinko. Then he said he did not want to sit next to me. Unable to restrain himself any longer, Rapp broke into laughter.

Many agents laughed at Hoover's book. *Tex Larkin,* who had grown up on a horse farm in Texas, said he hadn't seen horse shit piled so high since he left his daddy's ranch. *Masters of Deceit,* full of propaganda and copyright infringements, became the office joke.

I was happy that Hoover's book was an office joke. But I was mad as hell that Hoover had taken all the credit and that he received royalties on the book, which was a violation of federal law, while I had written the parts on Claude Lightfoot and Alfred Wagenknecht.

Each year, Hoover told Congress that his agents had given countless hours of voluntary service to the country without reimbursement, so, in 1955, Congress passed the Premium Overtime Act, requiring agents to be paid a 15% premium in overtime if they averaged overtime of one hour and twelve minutes a day in any one month out of a three-month period.

Hoover decided that his agents should average one hour and twelve minutes a day every month, not one month out of three, to qualify for the overtime pay. Thereafter, agents received promotions and office-of-preference transfers based on whether their overtime was above the office average. Agents who did not conform to the overtime standard were punished.

To stay within the office average overtime, agents falsified sign-in and sign-out times. In the morning, we arrived around 7 but signed in that we had arrived at 6, on the honor system, and then went out for breakfast. In the evening, we went to the local pub for drinks and then dinner, returning about 9 to sign out and go home. We did this to be above the office average.

Steve Conkling refused to play this game, and received several threats from his supervisor and from the Special Agent in Charge that severe administrative action would be taken if he did not conform. Conkling maintained his integrity.

Mr. Hoover, Associate Director Clyde Tolson, and Assistant Director in Charge of the Administrative Division John P. Mohr were furious with Conkling. A high-ranking officer in the U.S. Marine Corps Reserve who participated in weekend drills, Conkling was transferred to the only FBI field office without a U.S. Marine Corps Reserve unit in its territory. He resigned. This and other intimidation tactics of Hoover's FBI, such as the weight requirement, were pushing me more and more toward leaving the FBI.

Hoover's weight program specified that any agent who did not meet the weight requirements, regardless of the agent's size or build, was to receive severe administrative action.

Soon after Conkling resigned, agent *Rolf Accord*—six foot four inches tall and 235 pounds—was ordered to lose 30 pounds and bring his weight in line with Hoover's guidelines of 205 pounds for a man of six foot four inches with a large build. When the physical examiner, Dr. Silverman, wrote a personal letter to Hoover saying that he would not be responsible for Accord's health if Accord was ordered to lose any more weight, Hoover was furious, and ordered the Chicago office to change examination facilities.

I thought Hoover had taken leave of his senses. This meant that I now had to drive 120 miles round trip from Park Forest to the Great Lakes Naval Training Station at Great Lakes, Illinois, just to take an annual physical exam. Hoover's madness cost the taxpayer one full day of an agent's time. It cost about $11,000 a year in lost time in the 1950s for all agents in the Chicago office to get a physical exam at Great Lakes. In today's figures it would cost approximately $44,000, not counting transportation.

Agent *Randy Newsum*, who was five pounds overweight, was transferred to New Orleans, 912 miles from Chicago. Agent *Tom Langhorn*, who was fifteen pounds overweight, resigned under pressure and opened his own gourmet steak restaurant in Chesterton near Dune Acres, Indiana. Agent *Bill Laughing,* who was six pounds overweight, resigned and returned to Texas. I can name at least fifty other agents in the Chicago office who resigned.

By this time, I had decided to leave Chicago, and I wrote a letter, on October 15, 1959, to Mr. Hoover saying that I was available for transfer to the bureau's Spanish language school in Monterey, California.

Joe Culkin was furious. He said, "I can't recommend you because I need you here in Chicago. We have no replacement and you're doing a good job on the NPPR." When Culkin said he could not recommend me, I suddenly realized that he had planned this betrayal in 1958 when he suggested that I tell Hoover I was not interested in language school after buying the house in Dune Acres. I said, confused, "You don't need me now. The NPPR problem is all over. I took care of that last summer. Why can't you recommend me like you said you would last year?" Culkin refused to recommend me. Angrily, I sent my letter anyway.

I received a personal letter from J. Edgar Hoover dated October 22, 1959, on his blue print stationery with his signature in blue ink. Mr. Hoover was gratified that I had studied Spanish to render my services more valuable to the bureau. I read the letter expecting to see that I had been transferred to the Spanish language school in Monterey or to San Juan, Puerto Rico.

My heart nearly stopped as I read, "Unfortunately, I must advise you that I will not be able to grant your request. Your past performance in regard to matters requiring Spanish ability has been quite satisfactory, reflecting an adequate knowledge of this language at the present time. I am sure you can appreciate the fact that it would be inadvisable from both the bureau's standpoint and yours to select you for attendance at a Spanish School when your ability in this field is apparently already the equal of a graduate of such a school."

I knew instantly that Culkin had sent a horseshit comment to Hoover along with my letter.

I went to the Chief Clerk's office and asked *Marylin Lovely,* the Section Chief of the Administrative Files, to give me the correspondence on my letter to Mr. Hoover about Spanish school. She got up and without hesitation pulled open a file drawer and withdrew a file containing Culkin's comments that had gone to the bureau with my letter to Hoover. She handed me the file and said, "I wondered how soon you would come down here."

Culkin had written to Hoover that the Chicago office had no replacement for me and that I had handled my Spanish assignments in an exemplary manner. I submitted my resignation three days after my thirty-third birthday to be effective at the close of business on June 10, 1960. I asked for an autographed picture of J. Edgar Hoover. A veteran FBI agent, Al Mehegan, told me not to burn my bridges. Al said, "It is a cold world out there, Wes."

I did not know that the outside world could be as cold as Supervisor Joseph M. Culkin's office. After all the illegal break-ins Culkin and I had been through, I could not understand why he was giving me a royal screwing. If Culkin had been any other supervisor in the Chicago office or someone like Ewell C. Richardson in Memphis, I would have been on my way to a new career in a Spanish speaking office. Culkin had destroyed my dreams of criminal investigations in the FBI.

The day I left the Chicago office I received a letter from my fellow agents certifying that I was a member in good standing of "The Society of Culkin Rejects." I cherished that letter more than the signed photograph of Hoover.

Hoover lied about the turnover in the FBI, claiming it was less than one-half of one percent and lower than the industrial average. The FBI had 5,458 Special Agents in 1955. Resignations in Chicago alone, with 275 agents, averaged one agent per week, for a turnover rate of 18%. Twelve agents from Joseph Culkin's squad resigned in 1955, giving Culkin more than a 50% turnover.

I guessed from all this that Culkin was either a bad supervisor or that many other agents were fed up with the FBI. I knew one thing for sure, and it was that Hoover was a prevaricator.

Anne and I sold our house in Dune Acres and moved into an apartment at 900 North Lake Shore Drive. The view in the evening overlooking Michigan Avenue and Grant Park was like a thousand-dollar-a-night glimpse at heaven from some fancy resort hotel.

We had moved into an apartment so Anne could be close to Loyola University on Chicago Avenue where she attended courses for her master's degree in education. I audited several advanced accounting courses at Loyola in preparation for going to work with my older brother Thomas who was a certified public accountant in Riverside, California. Tom had offered me a partnership in his business. He had visions of naming his company Swearingen and Swearingen, Certified Public Accountants.

Tom was eleven years my senior. His wife, Tillie, worked in the office as a secretary and typed letters and tax returns. Our mother was Tom's office receptionist. Our father worked as a bookkeeper.

Tom was the oldest of five children and he had learned to boss us at an early age. After I moved to California in late 1960, I saw immediately that Tom had not changed his domineering ways because he often lost his temper with Tillie and Mother just as he had done when I was a kid. His attitude in the office was unprofessional.

I missed the freedom of being able to leave the office to conduct investigations and interview people. I soon tired of working on other individuals' income tax returns all day long without leaving my desk except for lunch or to go to the rest room. Tom was demanding and I had to keep track of my day in six-minute increments to be charged to a particular client. After one tax season I decided to try the FBI again, thinking I would be reinstated in some small office like Memphis where criminal investigations were the main line of work.

New agents from training school were never sent close to their home town. I thought that returning to Chicago would be impossible. Although I was tired of bag jobs, the Security Index, and writing security reports, I knew the FBI's criminal work was interesting and, if I could only be assigned to a small office, the return to the FBI would be rewarding.

Hoover accepted my request for reinstatement, but ordered me to report to Chicago on May 15, 1961. I was devastated. Anne was still in the apartment at 900 North Lake Shore Drive, but I did not want to see Joe Culkin ever again.

Special Agent in Charge James H. Gale greeted me upon my arrival. After a short discussion of how I had liked my brother's business, he said I was being assigned to Joseph Culkin's squad.

I thought of resigning again but decided to stay because I could not afford to be bouncing around from one job to another. My employment résumé would look terrible.

Chapter 6

Starting Over

A Time of Change

A lot of changes had taken place during my one-year absence from the FBI from June 1960 to May 1961. The office had moved from 212 West Monroe Street to the General Services Administration building at 536 South Clark Street, next to the Eisenhower Freeway. The new space had windows. Culkin's office was a glassed-in space about ten feet by ten feet. All the squad supervisors were in human fishbowls within their own squad area of a huge bull pen.

Joy McDuffy, one of my favorite stenographers, had been transferred to another office at her request. Before I had resigned, Joy had told me she had a choice of being promoted to a squad secretary or taking a transfer to Hawaii. One requirement for the squad secretary position with supervisor *John Walker* was that she had to have sex with Mr. Walker, a married man with five children. I suggested she take the transfer to Honolulu.

I stopped taking the FBI's rules and regulations so seriously.

Although Joseph M. Culkin supervised the Foreign Counterintelligence squad, which I had been assigned to, he was still preoccupied with issues such as overtime, time in the office, informant quotas, and time developing informants. When Culkin said, during one of his weekly squad conferences, that our squad had the lowest overtime average last month of any squad in the office, I could not resist saying, "That just proves you have the most honest squad in the office." The other agents burst into a brouhaha of laughter.

My new partner *Mike Sampson*'s approach to overtime was to sit in a bar and drink Cutty Sark Scots Whisky. He called it "contacting his informant."

I instantly liked Mike's approach to overtime. From the time we started drinking together, we had no trouble staying above the office average overtime. Culkin even smiled when, during his conferences, he read off the squad average overtime compared to the office average.

A few weeks before the annual inspection, Culkin called me into his office. He said, "Wes, you need to develop some informants for the forthcoming inspection." I said, "No problem," knowing that I could fake my way through the task.

Many agents took names from grave markers in the cemetery or names from the telephone book to refer to as potential informants in memos. I used names of janitors, bar tenders, and newspaper delivery men to open informant files just before the inspection. After the inspectors left town, I closed the files until next year. This was standard practice for most agents.

The long hours of surveillance during the years I had worked the Communist Party underground and was away from home, at times, from 3 A.M. to 11 P.M. to do bag jobs had strained my marriage to Anne. She had asked me once, during the peak years of my long days and nights, whether I would like a divorce. I flatly refused her suggestion because divorce was unheard of in my family. Years later, I knew it was time to break the family tradition, because the office average overtime was up to three and a half hours per day. I did not have a normal life with Anne because of the long hours. Hoover's demands were a strain on many marriages. I asked Anne in the fall of 1961 if she still wanted a divorce. Without any display of emotion she said, "Sure. When can you move out?"

Her cool quick reply startled me. Also, I had expected her to move since the apartment's lease was in my name. Anne was adamant about keeping the apartment. In a few days I found an efficiency apartment overlooking Lake Michigan on the top floor of our building. I moved into the new apartment with my handmade furniture and one single bed.

Anne immediately filed for divorce, charging me with desertion. I did not hire an attorney because I did not want to fight with her over anything, not even alimony. I did not want to embarrass Hoover or the bureau. I knew that if our divorce hit the news, I would be transferred to a disciplinary office.

That fall one of the hottest cases in FBI history began to unfold. It was not some Soviet spy defecting to the United States or a Mafia kingpin turning informant. Special Agent William W. Turner, a ten-year veteran of the FBI, had fired off a barrage of letters to members of Congress asking for *a congressional investigation of the FBI.*

My first inclination was to back Turner in his charges of FBI corruption, deceit, duplicity, fraud, and chicanery. My fellow agents convinced me that discretion was the better part of valor, so I did nothing but read the newspapers about how Hoover was denying all charges and was attempting to discredit Bill Turner. I had become a worthless piece of nothing without the guts to stand behind a fellow agent in his charges against Hoover and the FBI. For years I had trampled on the Constitution for Hoover and the FBI, I had disrespected the law, and yet I did nothing to expose the corruption when the opportunity presented itself. I was afraid to say or do what Turner had the guts to do. I wanted job security. I was ashamed of what I had become.

Hoover issued a communiqué to the field prohibiting any agent from contacting William Turner without prior bureau approval. This was Hoover's way of freezing out Turner.

Turner was forced to resign because of his allegations. Turner later wrote a book titled *Hoover's FBI: The Men and the Myth.*

Hoover made it clear to all agents that he would not tolerate any whistle-blowers in the FBI. Other agents and I were intimidated to the point that we did nothing to aid Turner, knowing all along that Turner was correct. After Turner's book was published, all agents were coerced into signing an agreement that they would not write a book about the FBI.

My divorce from Anne became final on Friday, May 18, 1962, just two days before my thirty-fifth birthday. The divorce did not tarnish my career. On Saturday I went to a New Members party at the Columbia Yacht Club in Chicago Harbor. I celebrated the divorce, my birthday, and my new yacht club membership.

At the yacht club, I met *Paula Goodfellow*. We fell in love and got engaged on Septmeber 15, 1962. We got married and I was immediately transferred.

Paula had married *Jonathan Goodfellow* in 1947. Jonathan had served five years in the military during World War II in the South Pacific. When Goodfellow had returned home, he had not liked the government's plans for political thought control. Jonathan had become a political activist just about the time he had married Paula. Also, Jonathan had supported Henry Wallace, the former vice president under Franklin D. Roosevelt who had formed the Progressive Party in 1948. Paula had been swept up in the political wave to elect Henry Wallace and to oppose the Broyles Bill. She soon had tired of Jonathan and his political activism and moved out of his apartment. Her divorce was final in 1951. But when I ran Paula's name through the Chicago FBI office indices, I found that as far as J. Edgar Hoover was concerned, Paula was the next best thing to a Russian spy.

I told supervisor Joe Culkin of my plans to marry Paula. After I gave him a briefing on Paula's background, Culkin said, "Caesar's wife must be above reproach."

I answered, "I'm not Caesar."

"Don't get smart. You know what I mean."

"No, I don't."

"What if she finds out what you do?"

"How is she going to do that? I was married to Anne for ten years. Not once did I tell her about bag jobs, mail openings at the post office, the Security Index, or the names of any of the cases I worked."

"Paula could embarrass the bureau," he replied.

Culkin thought Wallace's Progressive Party was a communist front organization and that all Wallace supporters were communists. I decided to ignore his blatant paranoia, and Paula and I were married on November 21, 1962, by a divorce court judge who was her friend. I notified Hoover of my marriage to Paula. I made Chicago my only office of preference. I expected to remain in Chicago for many years and enjoy yacht racing with Paula on Lake Michigan.

By return mail, Hoover transferred me to Louisville, Kentucky. I went to Culkin and asked, "What the hell is this?"

He answered, "Information in personnel files is Top Secret and Confidential."

Culkin wanted me off his squad and out of Chicago because he knew that I knew too many of the FBI's dark secrets and didn't trust me to avoid "pillow talk" with such a supposedly dangerous element as Paula.

C h a p t e r   7

Louisville

Home of the Kentucky Derby

Paula and I left Chicago during the first weekend in January 1963. We drove the 292 miles in my white 1959 Cadillac Sedan DeVille that I had bought used right after my divorce.

On Monday, January 7, 1963, I reported for duty in the Louisville Division, which covered the entire state of Kentucky. Kentucky is known as Blue Grass Country. Within the FBI, Louisville was known as a "country club" office. I did not know at the time why Hoover had sent me to a country club office after marrying someone like Paula Goodfellow.

Documents from my personnel file, which I obtained under the Freedom of Information Act of 1966 after I retired, reveal exactly why I had been transferred to Louisville. I had an inkling in 1963 of the reason, knowing Joseph Culkin as I did, but I did not know the details until 1979.

Joe Culkin had recommended an investigation of Paula for the purpose of determining whether her marriage to a Special Agent involved a security risk. The FBI conducted a complete investigation on Paula's family and relatives but found *no* information indicating that she or her family were security risks. Still, since Culkin had accused me of not having informed the FBI of Paula's background immediately upon learning of it, the bureau Inspector had recommended that I "be transferred to an office where security-type work is not as prominent a part of the office responsibilities as is the case in the Chicago area." It was also recommended that I not be sent a letter of congratulations on my recent marriage.

All the letters from the Chicago office to the bureau and other field offices concerning my marriage and Paula's background were written by "JMC," or Joseph M. Culkin. Culkin had tried his best to find something wrong with Paula so that I might be fired. Culkin never obtained his objective because there was nothing to find.

My marriage to Paula accomplished what I had not been able to do by studying Spanish, requesting Language School, or resigning and being reinstated—an assignment in an office that did primarily criminal work.

I was not in Louisville long before an opportunity to move up to grade GS-13 level presented itself. But before they would promote me, Paula and I had to move to Paintsville, in Appalachia, where I became the Senior Resident Agent.

Paintsville was the epitome of boondocks—which can be defined as an uninhabited area with thick natural vegetation, as a back-woods or marsh. The population of Paintsville was 2,000, counting all the dogs, cats, and chickens. Few persons moved to Paintsville. They most often moved away from Paintsville.

The first seven months in Paintsville were exciting because I did criminal investigations my way and I got results. I arrested two fugitives, single-handedly, one a prison escapee who said he would not be taken alive and the other an armed bank robber. No other FBI agent can claim that. With the help of one sheriff, I also arrested another prison escapee who had claimed he would not be taken alive. Single-handed arrests are a violation of FBI rules. I did not receive commendations for either single-handed arrest or the arrest with the sheriff, although the FBI had conducted a nationwide manhunt for all three men, and if these men had been arrested by a squad of FBI agents all the agents would have received commendations from Hoover.

Since Hoover was punishing me for marrying Paula, I could have become a goof-up and a goof-off, to show my resentment, but I did not. In fact, Hoover sent me four letters of commendation during my first year in exile for outstanding devotion to duty.

I soon got the hang of criminal investigations, the forms I had to fill out, and how to finagle statistics. I got credit for recovering a stolen car if the local police, sheriff, or the Kentucky State Police arrested anyone in a stolen car or if they found an abandoned stolen car. If an arrest was made, I took all the information, interviewed the suspect, and wrote a report for the U.S. Attorney in Lexington, who then prosecuted the suspect in federal court. I earned three statistics in this kind of case: 1) one car recovery; 2) a dollar recovery value for the car, usually listed at the retail price; and 3) one conviction. If there were two suspects in the stolen car, then I received two convictions. This was standard practice throughout the country. The local police did the work, and the FBI took the credit.

For some strange reason, young men from the boondocks of Appalachia in eastern Kentucky did not want to be killed in Vietnam. I did not blame them. The stories of death and destruction were enough to make anyone not want to be a part of the Vietnam fiasco. When the young men were drafted they soon deserted.

My job, like it or not, was to catch the deserters and return them to the appropriate military authorities. Deserter apprehensions were another one of Hoover's inflated statistics that he used to present to Congress. If the local police, sheriff, or the Kentucky State Police arrested a deserter, they notified me and I sent in the necessary information for them to get the $25 bounty paid by the Pentagon. The Kentucky State Police did not accept the reward, but I always received one statistic for a fugitive apprehended. It did not take long to catch on to the game of statistics. When I received the military's Form DD-553, declaring a man a deserter, I called the stockade at Fort Knox, Kentucky, to see if the deserter was in custody. If the Military Police picked up the man or if he returned on his own after visiting his friends or relatives and I could fill out the FBI deserter apprehension form before the agent covering Fort Knox received the information, then I got credit for a fugitive apprehension. I got about two a month by telephone. The other half dozen or so I arrested myself.

I had to prove my worth to the FBI in order to qualify for the grade GS-13 promotion that had been promised me in Louisville if I took the transfer to Paintsville. During the time I was in Paintsville, I had closed, in some months, almost 50% more cases than the office average for the State of Kentucky, which was no small feat. The only month that I was not above the office average was the period in September when I took two weeks leave.

Still, on March 11, 1963, I was passed over for promotion to GS-13. On September 25, 1963, I was again considered and passed over for promotion. The recommendations of the Louisville office had fallen on deaf ears at the bureau. In the mind of John P. Mohr, who was the Assistant Director of the Administrative Division, I was still a no-goodnik. However, in the following month, I uncovered a car theft ring, and was re-established as an above-average agent.

During the Louisville office Christmas party in December 1963, Special Agent Robert Peters, who was a member of Louisville's "palace guard" and a relief supervisor, danced with Paula. Peters told Paula that she was ruining my career and that she should get a divorce. Paula was in tears when she returned to the table. I was furious because apparently my personnel file, which was supposed to be Top Secret and Confidential, was privy to the entire Louisville Division.

Working criminal cases in a one-man resident agency made me forget the Security Index, Communist Index, Reserve Index, COMSAB, DETCOM, and the Communist Party. Even though Paula and I lived in a backward area of Appalachia, I loved the work I was doing. It was what I thought the FBI was supposed to be—a crime fighter.

My superiors were pleased with my work, so when the opportunity arose a year later, I requested a transfer to London, Kentucky. By letter dated January 25, 1965, Mr. Hoover transferred me to London, Kentucky. I was so happy to leave Paintsville that I reported for duty in London, Kentucky, on January 28, 1965.

In January 1966, the London Resident Agency became a training office for rookie agents just out of New Agents Training School. I was designated Senior Resident Agent and I began training new agents.

For three years, I worked in London, enjoying the criminal work and gaining commendations. I was flattered when, in January 1966, Mr. Hoover approved me as a bureau speaker. I was surprised with Hoover's confidence in me after what Bob Peters had said about Paula ruining my bureau career.

By 1968, I was ready to move on. My parents, who were both 78 in 1968, lived in Riverside, California. I had been away from my parents since 1951 and wanted to return to California to be close to them before they died. The FBI had a surplus of funds in 1968, so the Administrative Division began transferring agents to their office of preference rather than return the surplus funds to the U.S. Treasury.

But once again, the FBI's petty rules and regulations blocked me. I was passed over for a transfer to Los Angeles because my overtime, always selectively measured, was supposedly below the office average.

I applied for a transfer to New York. New York was easy to get. I liked working in London but I did not want to stand still for another royal screwing from the bureau when I had done nothing wrong. I received a transfer to New York City by return mail. I knew I would miss the Kentucky State Police. They were the best law enforcement agency I ever had the honor and privilege of working with.

But I was perplexed by the transfer. If Paula was such a security risk that I had to be transferred from Chicago to Appalachia in 1963, why was I granted a transfer to the spy capital of the world just five years later? I can only presume that my superiors in Louisville realized Paula was not a risk, that they knew I was an extremely capable investigator, and that they knew Joseph Culkin had fabricated the security risk story to Hoover because both Culkin and Hoover suffered from an illness I call xenophobic McCarthyism.

Paula and I had bought a 32-foot sailboat the year before and kept it on Lake Michigan in the Michigan City marina. We sailed as often as possible while in London. While in New York, we moved the boat to Milford, Connecticut and spent nearly every weekend on the boat during the summer months. It was great.

The New York office was much different from Memphis, Chicago, and Louisville. The agents in these latter offices were relatively hard workers. The New York office agents had more ways to goof off than you could imagine. Anthony Villano, author of *Brick Agent,* was correct in his assessment of the different classes of agents—the boozers, the jocks, the stock market investors, the movie goers, and the lovers.

The first few times I went to lunch near the office, I was shocked to see clerks, stenographers, and secretaries having Martinis and Manhattans with their lunches, in violation of Hoover's strict orders. For many of the agents the perfect day ended at noon in a neighborhood pub. The barroom agents were signed out by their buddies and picked up around six by their car pool.

John "Cement Head" Malone, who was the Assistant Director in Charge of the New York office, had supervisors monitor the sign-in register every morning to see that agents did not cheat on their overtime. When I saw this I thought I had made a mistake by moving to New York.

I soon learned that many agents worked about three hours in the morning shuffling papers and then left the office to go to the movies, check the stock market, meet their girlfriends, or whatever else they wanted to do for the rest of the day. It was called a "noon balloon" only if one quit work before noon to goof off for the rest of the day. Agents who took the noon balloon called the office in the evening to be signed out by the night clerk. This was how many agents maintained their overtime in New York City.

I was assigned to Criminal Division II. The New York office had four divisions including two criminal divisions, an administrative division and a security division. I was given a preference of squads and I chose the car squad because I liked stolen car cases and I thought the recovery statistics in New York would be good.

Hoover used recovery statistics to impress Congress and to obtain an ever increasing annual budget.

When Dick Baker, the agent in charge of Division II whom I had worked with in Chicago, told me that the car squad had not made a single arrest in the past year, I was amazed.

The following week agent Jerry Smith arrived from the Birmingham office and asked to be assigned to the car squad. Because Jerry and I were new to the squad, we teamed up and went to work. Jerry was one of the best agents I ever worked with, but he was a workaholic. We never took the noon balloon—we often worked until 9 P.M.

One morning we received a call from a member of a car theft ring who had had a falling out with his buddies. The caller gave us the location of a stolen car in Brooklyn. We verified the theft and immediately drove to the scene. We spotted two suspects driving the stolen silver Corvette toward the motor vehicle registration office with the stolen license plates still on the car. We arrested the suspects and took them to the U.S. magistrate. Dick Baker was pleased with our performance, and so we each received an incentive award of $150 from Mr. Hoover.

Within a few months Jerry and I had discovered a number of car rings operating in New York, and we had made several more arrests. Eventually, each agent on the car squad was assigned at least one car ring case. Some agents had two.

The car squad also handled bombing matters. Because I was good at shuffling papers and had had experience in coal mine bombings in Kentucky, I was assigned all bombing matters in New York City. In 1969, I solved the anti-Castro Cuban bombings in New York with the assistance of agents in Los Angeles and Miami. No sooner did the anti-Castro Cuban bombings end then a group calling themselves the Crazies, headed by Sam Melville, bombed several buildings in New York City, including the Federal Office Building at 26 Federal Plaza. The case was assigned to me. With the cooperation of a special bomb squad and the entire New York office and the New York City police department, the bombings were solved and Sam Melville and his cohorts were arrested and convicted in 1970.

Fortunately for the people of New York City, Sam Melville was killed during the Attica Prison riots in 1971, with bombs strapped to his body.

Mr. Hoover sent me an incentive award of $200 for my part in solving the Melville bombings. Two months after Melville's conviction, Hoover transferred me to Los Angeles, my office of preference, the one I truly wanted and for which I had waited nearly twenty years.

I had sold the 1961 Cadillac convertible after arriving in New York City, so we had to fly. In a style typical of the way many New York City agents operated, I made reservations for two first-class seats to Los Angeles on the new American Airlines 747 Jumbo Jet.

Chapter 8

"There Are No Weathermen in LA"

Our plane touched down at Los Angeles International Airport as gently as a ping-pong ball falling on a feather bed. Of course, with all the complimentary twelve-year-old Chivas Regal Scotch Whisky I had drunk in first class, the plane could have made a belly landing and I would not have noticed the difference. I had drunk more than usual because I was returning home to California where I would be close to my parents after nearly twenty years and I was leaving the likes of Joseph Culkin and the memories of my meaningless exiled transfer to Appalachia 2,000 miles behind.

Tuesday, May 12, 1970, I checked into the Los Angeles FBI office. After a tour of the office, I asked to be assigned to the Weatherman Squad.

In New York, I had visited the scene of the bomb explosion that had killed Diana Oughton, Ted Gold, and Terry Robbins, all of who were members of the Weatherman Underground Organization. I wanted to try my hand at finding these smartish college kids with PhDs, like Bernardine Dohrn, who spelled America with a K.

I was assigned to Security Squad Number 1 (S-1), the "Old Left." Our assignment was much like the one I had had in Chicago writing reports on the aging Communist Party members who were on the Security Index. I was disheartened to find the same petty rules and routine corruption in the Los Angeles office that I had seen in Chicago and New York.

Unlike Assistant Director John Malone, who watched agents sign in and who checked the coffee shops in the morning and afternoon to be sure agents were not drinking coffee on bureau time, Special Agent in Charge Wesley Grapp was more interested in the important things of office administration, like checking the garage in the morning for dusty cars. He walked through the office to be sure agents did not hang suit coats on the backs of their chairs. We were to keep ash trays in the desk when out of the office, and we were not to leave work boxes on the desk. Telephone books had to be stacked with the telephone next to the books, not on top of a book. Chairs had to be pushed into the chair well, not left askew.

Grapp did not like an agent to have a mustache. The late Larry Schlapp grew some fuzz on his upper lip after Hoover died. Grapp sent him on a desert road trip in July in a car without air conditioning. Larry was clean-shaven when he returned.

In general, agents cheated and lied to conform to FBI requirements. Following the Los Angeles Watts riots in August 1965, someone in "Sleepy Hollow," the field agent's term for the headquarters in Washington, D.C., dreamed up the idea that if each agent in Los Angeles had a "ghetto" informer, such riots could be avoided! Each agent was required to have one black informant living in the Watts area who could report on any potential unrest. If any unrest developed, then the FBI could alert the Los Angeles police department, who would then swoop down with hundreds of uniformed officers wearing riot gear to quell any uprising.

John Keet, whom I had met nineteen years earlier in Memphis when we were first office agents, asked me if I needed a "ghetto" informer. Naively, I said I did. As it turned out, Keet's "informer" was phony.

Keet said that all I had to do was fill out the FD-209 contact form every month to keep the file posted and up to date. Keet laughed, "You didn't think Hoover's ghetto informant program was for real, did you?"

It was déjà vu. It was disheartening to see what nearly twenty years in Hoover's FBI had done to Keet's integrity and to see a mirrored reflection of myself and to know we both had fallen into the bottomless pit of fraud and corruption.

I took Keet's ghetto informer and filled out fraudulent FD-209s for many years until the idiotic program was discontinued in time to avoid the General Accounting Office audit of FBI files, which had begun in 1974. The lack of supervision of the Weatherman Squad from 1970 to 1977 was chaos. Incidents I set forth in this chapter show why the FBI in Los Angeles was unable to arrest a Weatherman fugitive in six years. The cost to taxpayers was $4 million just in agents' salaries.

My work on Weatherman cases further exposed me to FBI mismanagement and corruption—in one case, leading to the imprisonment of innocent people.

One week after I started to work for Security Coordinator of the Security Section Bill Nolan, whom I considered incompetent, he handed me a sabotage case he had been holding for a week. Sabotage was one of the FBI's highest-priority cases and required a full field investigation and a written report to the bureau within two weeks.

I immediately made an appointment to meet Detective Donald Day of the Los Angeles Police Department Criminal Conspiracy Section, who had been working on the case. Don Day was naive about the Weatherman Underground Organization and I was naive about Los Angeles, so we had a common ground. Detective Day had done all the routine paperwork of obtaining a California driver's license of the man who had bought fifty pounds of dynamite and blasting caps at a store in Tucson, Arizona, on May 4, 1970.

The store owner in Tucson became leery of the man from California when he said he needed fifty pounds of dynamite and blasting caps to blow some tree stumps. The man furnished a California driver's license in the name of William Allan Friedman. When Friedman left with the dynamite, the store owner telephoned the police.

Day found no record of Friedman except at the Department of Motor Vehicles. He obtained a driver's license photograph of Friedman. The license address checked out to a Robert Gottlieb and Susan Sutheim. The car Friedman used was registered to Terri Ann Volpin.

Weatherman names were as familiar to me as the presidents of the United States, from my work in New York. I said to Day, "Hell, these are Weathermen."

The Weatherman organization was a militant group of several dozen college students from the radical organization known as Students for a Democratic Society (SDS). The Weathermen, led by Bernardine Rae Dohrn, who had a Doctor of Law degree, opposed the American establishment and denounced the largest of U.S. companies as fascist. Dohrn had attracted the FBI's attention during a violent confrontation with Chicago police in 1968 that resulted in dozens of arrests.* Many of the demonstrators became fugitives when they did not show up for their trial in 1969.

Don Day gave me a copy of Friedman's photograph. He said he would get a copy of the driver's license fingerprint. When I got back to the office, I took out all the photographs of the Weatherman fugitives and compared them with the photo of Friedman. William Allan Friedman had a full beard. It was difficult to compare his photo with those who were clean shaven. I divided the face in thirds. The head and eyes looked like Weatherman Identification Order fugitive John Fuerst. Identification Orders (IO) are the posters one sees in the U.S. Post Office of wanted criminals with the fugitive's photograph, fingerprints, description, and the history of the crime committed printed in bold type.

I went to Bill Nolan's office and told him I suspected "Friedman" was Fuerst. Nolan leaned back in his chair and puffed on his stick-like Tiparillo cigar, which he held between his teeth. With both hands he lightly stroked the short strands of hair on his otherwise bald head. After titillating himself with his stubby hair for several seconds, he grinned and said, "Wes, we don't have any Weathermen in the Los Angeles area."

"I know Friedman is Fuerst. Even with the heavy disguise in his driver's license photograph—his features stand out."

Nolan smiled and took a long drag on his Tiparillo. "Wes, you don't understand. There are no Weathermen in Los Angeles."

After the explosion in New York City in March, where three Weathermen had been accidentally killed, Hoover had ordered each major office to form a Weatherman squad and assign to those squads agents who had a proven record of fugitive apprehensions.

---

* The FBI had informers in the Weatherman organization who acted as *agent provocateurs.* The informers helped incite the Weathermen to riot against the police and the establishment in Chicago. The ensuing demonstrations, from October 8-11, 1968, became known as the "Days of Rage," when top Weatherman leaders were arrested by the Chicago police, just as the FBI had hoped.

Nolan, whom I considered to be a pompous ass, had told Hoover there were no Weathermen in Los Angeles, and therefore Los Angeles would not be forming a Weatherman squad.

I responded to Nolan angrily. I said, "I don't care what you told the bureau. There are Weathermen all over Venice. The address on Friedman's license is where two New York Weathermen Security Index subjects live, Robert Gottlieb and Susan Sutheim. The car Friedman used is registered to Terri Ann Volpin, 2201 Ocean Front Walk. That place is crawling with hippies."

Since Gottlieb and Sutheim were missing Security Index subjects from New York, I sent an airmail letter to the New York office advising them of the residence of Gottlieb and Sutheim. I requested that New York notify the bureau and forward appropriate copies of corrected Security Index cards to the bureau and Los Angeles.

Detective Day called me when he had received the driver's license fingerprint on Friedman. Day came to the FBI office, where I gave him a large package of Weatherman fugitive Identification Orders and about a hundred photographs of Weathermen who had attended what they called their "War Council" in December 1969 in Flint, Michigan, where the Weathermen formed their underground organization known as the WUO. The photographs included background information and physical descriptions. Don Day was happy with what I had given him. I was hysterically happy with the fingerprint of Friedman, which was positively identified as John Fuerst's.

Bill Nolan did not want to believe this, because he had put his career on the line when he told Hoover there were no Weathermen in Los Angeles. Nolan was devastated.

By the time I had convinced Nolan that Friedman was Fuerst, John Fuerst had slipped quietly out of Los Angeles with the dynamite. The six months of telephone toll records on Robert Gottlieb and Susan Sutheim that I had obtained had established that they had made no calls to any Weathermen that we could identify. With Nolan's refusal to believe in the presence of any Weathermen, the investigation seemed dead-ended. It was frustrating to see someone with Nolan's incompetence in charge of coordinating domestic intelligence in the Los Angeles field division. Nolan was Grapp's favorite supervisor, and Grapp was Hoover's favorite Special Agent in Charge. There was nothing I could do without rocking the boat and possibly being transferred out of Los Angeles.

Bill Nolan, the quintessential clerk in agent's clothing, said he wanted me to open new cases on 200 of the 400 phone numbers that Gottlieb and Sutheim had called—to places such as the library, restaurants, and dry cleaners.

Since I had documentary proof of several Weathermen and a Weatherman IO fugitive in the Los Angeles area with fifty pounds of dynamite, Nolan decided to form a Weatherman squad, just as Hoover had ordered him to do seven months earlier. I knew Nolan's procrastination had put us a half year behind the fugitives, but I had hoped that we could catch up to them. Most Weatherman fugitives had more years of formal education than the average FBI agent, and had established an underground network fashioned after the communist underground of the 1950s, so I knew we were facing a serious challenge.

With 200 telephone number cases we had enough of a caseload to assign about twenty agents to the nineteenth new squad in the Los Angeles office, which we called Security Squad Number 19 or S-19. Hoover had authorized the new squad in September 1970 with experienced agents to apprehend the Weatherman fugitives, but Nolan did not obey Hoover's orders. Many of the twenty agents Nolan assigned had no experience in locating and arresting fugitives, and some were just out of training school. I said to myself, "My god, this is going to be a fiasco." As it turned out, the younger agents often played volleyball on the Venice beach with airline stewardesses, cruised the campus of the University of California at Santa Barbara, or otherwise entertained themselves, and we did not catch a single fugitive in six years.

One reason Bill Nolan wanted more cases and more squads was so he could help his friend Wesley G. Grapp become the West Coast Director in Charge of the Los Angeles office and have the same status as John Malone in New York City. Nolan had aspirations of becoming the Special Agent in Charge of the Security Division in Los Angeles in an effort to increase his retirement benefits.

The supervisor of S-19, *Tom Kerr*, was approaching retirement age. He had been a good investigator in his day, but now he was a womanizer and a boozer.

My August 21, 1970 memorandum opening 200 new telephone cases included the Narcotics Prevention Project, the *Los Angeles Times*, Western Airlines, Cafe Figard, Airmotive Services, Inc., Nationwide Investment Corp., Penn and Quill Motor Hotel, California Institute of the Arts, the Los Angeles Public Library, the Los Angeles County Hospital, several local movie theaters, and the American Civil Liberties Union.*

Believe it or not, some agents were able to milk these telephone cases for nearly a year under supervisor Tom Kerr without reports to the bureau. When Edward S. Miller, convicted in 1980 for authorizing bag jobs against the Weatherman Underground Organization, inspected the Los Angeles office in April 1971, he prepared only one substantive write-up for the 200 cases I had opened. Miller's write-up, dated April 20, 1971, was on case number 100-76009, which was already eight months old. Even after Miller's substantive write-up, the case remained open for another five months in violation of rules and regulations. This is significant because it establishes the fact that the Los Angeles office was flaunting bureau rules and regulations and operated in a state of sustained mediocrity for years regarding Weatherman fugitive investigations. I am sure that several thousand FBI agents will find this hard to believe, but I have documented it, and all they have to do is look at the record, if it has not been shredded.

Instead of looking for John Fuerst, I was swimming in paper work because Bill Nolan wanted Terri Ann Volpin and nearly a dozen of her friends added to the Security Index just because Fuerst had borrowed Volpin's car.

---

* The American Civil Liberties Union case, Los Angeles file number 100-76052, a "security matter and subversive" classification, remained open for active investigation from August 21, 1970 until January 21, 1971, without a written report. This was a substantive error in violation of bureau rules and regulations. Although the case was officially "closed" in January 1971, the FBI continued to monitor the activities of the ACLU through this file until as late as April 24, 1975, when I last reviewed the Los Angeles file. This case should have been written up in the Inspector's Report to Hoover during the 1971 office inspection, but it was not.

On October 8, 1970, Bernardine Rae Dohrn, an Identification Order Weatherman fugitive and leader of the Weatherman Underground Organization, declared war on "Amerika" to mark the third anniversary of the death of Ché Guevara, the Cuban revolutionary who had been killed in Bolivia. Dohrn announced in a taped message that a "fall offensive of youth resistance will spread from Santa Barbara to Boston, back to Kent and Kansas." Bernardine continued, "Now we are everywhere, and next week families and tribes will attack the enemy around the country. It is our job to blast away the myths of the total superiority of *The Man.*"

By 6:00 the next morning, I was on my way to see the damage done from a bomb placed against the outside wall of the Santa Barbara National Guard Armory, Santa Barbara, California. I knew it was the work of an amateur because all the force of the dynamite blew in the line of least resistance, away from the wall. If the dynamite had been placed in a hole in a wall and tightly packed, the whole building could have gone up. As it was, the explosion site was barely visible from the street. I suspected John Fuerst, but I could not prove it.

Many FBI agents considered J. Edgar Hoover as *The Man.* We believed Bernardine Dohrn was referring to Hoover when she said she would blast away the myths of his total superiority. Hoover was outraged by Dohrn's scurrilous attack, and ordered Bernardine Dohrn added to the FBI's Ten Most Wanted list, also known as the Top Ten.

Bernardine Dohrn was the fourth woman to be added to the Ten Most Wanted list. She was in good company. Angela Yvonne Davis had been added on August 17, 1970 and arrested two months later. Susan Edith Saxe had been added on October 17, 1970. She was apprehended March 27, 1975. Katherine Anne Power had been added on October 17, 1970 and removed August 15, 1985, because the FBI could not find her. Power surrendered to authorities in 1993.

The average time on the Top Ten list is 157 days. Dohrn remained a fugitive until the charges were dismissed over three years later in 1973. The dismissal came in federal court in Detroit, when the U.S. Attorney General said the government could not disclose details of the surveillance without jeopardizing national security. This is the government's double-tongued way of saying that information culled from the illegal wiretaps and illegal bag jobs could not be used in a court of law and that Hoover, the FBI, and the Department of Justice would be embarrassed if a trial took place.

After Dohrn declared war on "Amerika," the Internal Security Division of the Department of Justice decided it was time to help the FBI. The Department of Justice held a grand jury session on John Fuerst and the five people living at 2201 Ocean Front Walk, one of whose car Fuerst had used, later to become known as the "Tucson Five."

I was opposed to the grand jury for two reasons: one, the publicity would chase the Weatherman fugitives from the Los Angeles area, and, two, the grand jury could not ethically charge John Fuerst or the five people living in Venice with any crime. It is not a crime to buy dynamite in Arizona. It is not a crime to live in a house in Venice, California.

A federal grand jury is a one-sided affair where the U.S. Attorney General presents information to twelve people to get the jury to return an indictment. The grand jury does not decide whether a person is guilty or innocent, just whether there should be a trial so that a different jury can decide the guilt or innocence of a person after hearing evidence from the prosecution and the defense. The grand jurists most often believe that the government has a case; otherwise the government would not bother with a presentation for an indictment.

I had gone to Tucson to follow the grand jury activities and to report back to Bill Nolan immediately if anyone told of the whereabouts of any Weatherman supporters or Weatherman fugitives.

Guy Goodwin was in charge of a new unit in the Department of Justice called the Special Litigation Unit. Goodwin's aim in using the grand jury system was to compel witnesses to testify against their friends with the threat of jail if they did not comply.

After each morning and afternoon session, Goodwin, his assistant, and I got together to discuss what had gone on. Goodwin needed me because I was the only FBI agent who knew firsthand the complete story of Fuerst, Volpin, Gottlieb, Sutheim, the UCLA students at 2201 Ocean Front Walk, the Weatherman bombings and the Weatherman fugitives. We had breakfast and lunch together. We relaxed at dinner with a few Margaritas, salsa and chips, and great food at Tucson's finest Mexican restaurants.

Goodwin's presentation of John Fuerst's purchase of dynamite and blasting caps resulted in an indictment. When John Fuerst surrendered to the charges in Tucson nine years later, the federal judge dismissed the case for lack of merit.

Goodwin knew he did not have a case on Fuerst, so he played the tough guy with the innocent "Tucson Five." Goodwin attempted to develop a broad view of West Coast Weatherman activities through the subpoenaed witness, Terri Ann Volpin, and her friends, none of whom were permitted an attorney in the courtroom.

Goodwin asked Volpin and her friends questions like: Where were you employed during 1970? By whom and for how long? How much were you paid during the year?

He demanded they tell the grand jury every place they had gone, with whom, their means of transportation, and whom they had visited when they had gone out of town during 1970. Goodwin wanted them to describe every occasion during 1970 when they had been in contact with, attended meetings of, or been any place when any individual spoke whom they knew to be associated or affiliated with the Students for a Democratic Society, the Weatherman organization, the Communist Party, or any other organization advocating revolutionary overthrow of the United States by force and violence.

Goodwin asked these questions of mere witnesses, people the FBI had under investigation but who had not committed a crime. Their only crime, so to speak, was living at 2201 Ocean Front Walk. Terri Volpin's only mistake was in loaning her car to John Fuerst, who drove it to Tucson, Arizona, to buy dynamite. The FBI could not prove that the "Tucson Five" knew who Fuerst really was. We never did establish that Fuerst took the car keys from Volpin. Robert Gottlieb or Susan Sutheim could have borrowed the car and then given the keys to John Fuerst.

That did not matter to Guy Goodwin. After the "Tucson Five" refused to answer his ridiculous questions by taking the Fifth, Goodwin gave them full (transactional) immunity by the district court. When they again refused to answer his questions, Goodwin had them thrown in the slammer for contempt of court, beginning in early November 1970. The conventional civil contempt sentence meant that each of the "Tucson Five" would remain in jail for the life of the grand jury (up to eighteen months), which in this case was until March 1971.

I felt sorry for the "Tucson Five," but my personal feelings made no difference. If I had made an official objection to the grand jury proceedings, I would have been replaced. By being there, I watched what happened and I knew what the American judicial system had done in the name of justice.

On March 25, when the five witnesses were released from jail, they were presented with subpoenas to appear before the grand jury starting on April 7, 1971. When I heard that the "Tucson Five" were going to be jailed for a second time, I went into Nolan's office and shouted, "I'm not going to be a part of this bullshit charade of justice for a second time."

Nolan smiled and said, "I'll send *Dimitri Tyne*. He needs a vacation in Tucson."

The kangaroo inquisition proved to be a failure because the five "witnesses" knew nothing of the whereabouts of the Weatherman underground support people or the Weatherman fugitives.

Nolan desperately wanted and needed a fugitive statistic, which was a fugitive arrest, to prove his superiority over other offices with Weatherman squads such as Chicago and New York. He would have recommended himself for at least a $500 cash award for his outstanding supervision if we had arrested John Fuerst.

Nolan ordered *Wendell Stone* and me to do a black bag job on Gottlieb and Sutheim at 1922 Pacific Avenue, without bureau approval. *Kobe Kyoto* was our lookout. We found nothing about any of the Weatherman underground support people or the Weatherman fugitives. Then Nolan ordered Stone, Tyne, Kyoto, and me to do a bag job on Elizabeth Stanley in the Silver Lake area of Los Angeles. We found nothing on the Weathermen or the fugitives.

In 1971, other agents on Squad 19 bagged the offices of Ken Cloke, a National Lawyers Guild attorney who worked at the legal aid office in Venice, California, and who counseled some of the "Tucson Five" witnesses during their inquisition by Guy Goodwin of the Department of Justice. They also bagged Barry Litt's offices, who also counseled some of the "Tucson Five." I do not know what happened to Ken Cloke. Mr. Litt is a member of the California Attorneys for Criminal Justice and is practicing law in Los Angeles.

Other Squad 19 agents bagged the offices of attorney Leslie H. Abramson, a suspected legal consultant for members of the Students for a Democratic Society and for the Weatherman Underground Organization. These law offices were burglarized by FBI agents in an effort to learn the whereabouts of Weatherman fugitives such as Bernadine Dohrn, but nothing to indicate the fugitives whereabouts was found in any of the law offices. In 1989, Leslie Abramson became president of the California Attorneys for Criminal Justice, an organization formed to improve the quality and administration of justice in California, and she is now a prominent defense attorney in Los Angeles.

We bagged Elizabeth Stanley twice more to no avail. I was told that other agents had bagged the law offices of Bar Sinister, a law firm in Los Angeles, and found nothing on the Weathermen or the fugitives.

Kerr and another supervisor, *Ray Hitt*, who were bag job experts from the 1950s, did a black bag job in July 1971 on Donald Mohs in Santa Barbara, California. Donald Mohs was using a California driver's license in the name of a deceased infant. Cril Payne, who wrote *Deep Cover,* Cril's sidekick "Crane," several other agents, and I had Mohs under surveillance while Kerr and Hitt broke into Mohs' house.

Of all the bag jobs and surveillances that Security Squad Number 19 performed, only the bag job on Donald Mohs was successful. Mohs was not a Weatherman, and he most likely had not heard of the Weatherman underground. But Mohs was actually Albert K. Field, an alleged college professor and an Arizona bail jumper from a marijuana-smuggling charge. Field was arrested and returned to Arizona, where he was convicted and served jail time.

I was beginning to plan for retirement even though it was six years away. Paula and I wanted a sailboat large enough to go long-distance cruising. We worked out a deal on a custom ordered forty-three-foot racing yacht, or Columbia 43, that slept eight people, but in order to make the monthly payments we had to move from our apartment in Marina Del Rey onto the boat. We sold all our furniture and moved onto the boat in a slip at the Bar Harbor Marina. Since I already had an address for the apartment on Via Marina Way, it was simple enough to give Hoover a change of address just across the street in the Bar Harbor marina. The boat slips had mail boxes and Hoover thought I was moving to a different apartment.

Hoover had a rule that special agents could not live in a trailer park. His rules did not say anything about living on a boat in a marina and I did not want to ask him if I could live on a boat. Hoover died a year later and many rules were relaxed. Even the weight limits were relaxed. My new desirable weight limit went from 190 pounds up to 205 pounds.

In December 1971, I was transferred to Security Squad Number 2, known as the racial squad. I was transferred because I had brought to supervisor Tom Kerr's attention the fact that several of his agents were cheating on their expense vouchers which were being routed through the Confidential fund via the John Fuerst case. Kerr asked me if I wanted to make my complaint official and I said, "No." I told Kerr it was just a word to the wise to be alert for inspection. In response, he transferred me to the racial squad, which I had told him I would hate to work for, since it was common knowledge that the supervisor of the racial squad was a racist who hated African Americans.

I remained on the racial squad until I had a problem with supervisor *Dred Scott*. Scott and I had a parting of the ways when I was attempting to develop a black man as an informant. One of Hoover's qualifications for a racial informant was that the potential informer had to have a criminal record. When I told Scott that the man had never been arrested, he blurted out, "Every black man ought to be in jail."

I replied, in disgust, "I didn't know I was working for a damned Gestapo skin head racist."

It was not long before I was transferred back to the Weatherman squad. During the time I served on the racial squad I learned how the FBI had arranged to assassinate members of the Black Panther Party by using hit men in the United Slaves organization, a black cultural nationalist organization based in southern California, who were FBI informers. I learned how the FBI had neutralized the charismatic leader of the Los Angeles Black Panther Party, Elmer "Geronimo" Pratt, by framing him for murder.

Chapter 9

The Black Panther Party

The racial squad investigated the Black Panther Party, the Black Liberation Army, the United Slaves, and other black organizations that were unacceptable to J. Edgar Hoover. The S-2 also investigated various white hate groups such as the American Nazi Party and the Sheriff's Posse Comitatus. It also investigated a very small group of young Hispanic political activists known as the Brown Berets.

The Black Panther Party was established as the Black Panther Party for Self-Defense in the San Francisco Bay area by two Merrit College students, Huey Newton and Bobby Seale, in October 1966. The Black Panthers had a ten-point program that resembled a political platform for a member of Congress or a presidential candidate. Its demands included freedom, power to determine the destiny of their community, full employment, the end to robbery by the white man of their community, decent housing, education that taught black history, exemption of black men from military service, an immediate end to police brutality and the murder of black people, freedom for black men in jail, fair trials in court by a jury of their peers as defined by the U.S. Constitution, and peace. The Black Panthers' platform was legal, but their ten-point program was unacceptable to Hoover and his all-white FBI.

By 1967, the Black Panther Party had organized a free breakfast program for black children and offered free health care to ghetto residents. They also had a community education project and an anti-heroin campaign.

In February 1968, Bobby Seale and Eldridge Cleaver planned the merger of the Black Panther Party with the Student Nonviolent

Coordinating Committee (SNCC). Stokely Carmichael was designated as honorary prime minister of the Panthers, H. Rap Brown as minister of justice, and James Forman as minister of foreign affairs.

FBI officials saw a strengthening coalition within the black community that they felt had to be stopped immediately. The FBI framed Stokely Carmichael as an informer for the CIA by planting an informant report in his car where other members could find it, with the help of another FBI informer. The report was discovered and the Panthers sent a "hit team" after Carmichael, who as a result departed immediately for an extended period in Africa.

The FBI's COINTELPRO had successfully neutralized the coalition between the Panthers and the Student Nonviolent Coordinating Committee, instigated by Hoover's paranoia of African Americans, but the Panthers were gaining respect in the black community across the country. Hoover wanted the Black Panther Party neutralized immediately, one way or the other.

In November 1968, Hoover wrote to the various FBI field offices in cities with growing Panther organizations that a serious struggle was developing between the Panthers and the United Slaves organization. Hoover wrote that the struggle had reached such proportions that it was taking on the aura of gang warfare with threats of murder.

Then, in December 1968, Hoover ordered these offices to submit letters every two weeks outlining the counterintelligence measures that were being taken to neutralize the Black Panther Party. These bi-weekly letters were to list the accomplishments achieved in attacking the Panthers.

Soon after I had been assigned to the Los Angeles racial squad, I was told by a fellow agent, *Joel Ash*, that another agent on the squad, *Nick Galt,* had arranged for Galt's informers in the United Slaves to assassinate Alprentice Carter, the Panther's Los Angeles minister of defense, and John Huggins, the deputy minister of information. Following Galt's instructions, informants George Stiner and Larry Stiner shot them to death on the UCLA campus on January 17, 1969.

I had thought Joel Ash had been kidding me because this was beyond any corruption or wrongdoing that I had witnessed or heard of by FBI agents.

I later reviewed the Los Angeles files and verified that the Stiner brothers were FBI informants. I knew they must be real informants, even though the informant programs that I knew about in Chicago and Los Angeles were approximately 75% phony, because Hoover wanted the Panthers in jail or dead. That was why he had ordered bi-weekly reports from the field about the campaign against the Black Panther Party.

Darthard Perry, a self-admitted and publicly acclaimed informer for the FBI, filed an affidavit in a Black Panther Party lawsuit against the government charging that he knew that the United Slaves members who were responsible for the murders of the Panthers were FBI informers. Perry claims that the murders committed by the Stiner brothers, who were convicted and sent to jail in 1969, and their subsequent escape in the 1974 prison break from San Quentin, were engineered by the FBI. I then discovered the unthinkable, that FBI informants had actually been instructed by FBI agents to assassinate several other Black Panther members.

As of 1992, the Stiner brothers were still listed as fugitives. Either the FBI has disposed of the Stiners or they are in the FBI's Witness Protection Program. I know that Darthard Perry was an FBI informant and that he is telling the truth about the FBI.*

United Slaves member *Bill Stark,* an FBI informer, shot and killed Panther member *Al Holt,* another FBI informer, on March 14, 1969.**

---

* From my work with false identification on the Weathermen in 1971, I learned that the FBI had arranged for Perry to give Elmer Geronimo Pratt phony identification in 1972 from the Weatherman files. Perry was to assist Pratt in a jail break so that the FBI could track Pratt's contacts in the black nationalist underground, via the National Crime Information Center (NCIC). If Pratt were arrested after the jail break while using the phony identification, the FBI would have short-circuited a police inquiry through NCIC. Later, the FBI would do an inocuous follow-up interview with the arresting officer to determine Pratt's city of operation and then would have developed, through informers, the black nationalist underground contacts in that city.

** According to a May 26, 1970 memo from the Los Angeles Special Agent in Charge to the Director, the racial squad "is aware of the mutually

The Los Angeles files revealed that a Panther member was shot by a United Slaves member on March 17, 1969. Julius Carl Butler, an informer for the Los Angeles Police Department and the FBI for several years, retaliated by shooting up the home of James Doss. United Slaves member Jerry Horne shot and killed Panther member John Savage on May 23, 1969. On August 14, 1969, United Slaves members wounded two Black Panthers. Sylvester Bell, another Panther member, was killed by FBI informers in the United Slaves on August 15, 1969.

The FBI eagerly took credit for this high degree of unrest in a communication to Hoover that stated, "It is felt that a substantial amount of the unrest is directly attributable to this program," referring to the FBI's counterintelligence program, code named COINTELPRO. The FBI has denied any wrongdoing, but agents have told me what happened and I have read the files of the Los Angeles FBI office.

Panther Leader Elmer Pratt was framed by the FBI and the Los Angeles Police Department in 1972, and he is now serving life in prison.

After four months on the racial squad, our supervisor, Dred Scott, held a squad conference to brief the new members, including me, on the forthcoming May 1972 trial of Elmer "Geronimo" Pratt for murder.

Elmer Pratt had become the leader of the Panthers in Los Angeles after the assassination of Alprentice Carter and John Huggins. Pratt had served two tours of duty in Vietnam as a decorated paratrooper and he had received an honorable discharge in 1968. He then had attended UCLA on the GI Bill. Soon after Pratt had joined the Panthers, the FBI had arranged to have his veteran's benefits cut off in November 1968.

At the squad conference in April 1972, Dred Scott said that Kenneth Olsen and Caroline Olsen had been attacked on a tennis court in Santa Monica on December 18, 1968, by two black men. Caroline was

hostile feelings harbored between the organizations and the first opportunity to capitalize on the situation will be maximized. It is intended that U.S. Inc. will be appropriately and discreetly advised of the time and location of BPP activities in order that the two organizations might be brought together and thus grant nature the opportunity to take her due course."

shot and killed. Kenneth had tentatively identified several persons from photographs shown to him by the Santa Monica Police Department and positively identified one person from a photograph.

Scott told us how the Los Angeles police department (LAPD) had explained to Mr. Olsen that Pratt was the leader of the Panthers in Los Angeles and that a car like Pratt's had been seen in the area of the tennis court on the night of the shooting. Scott said that, Olsen positively identified Geronimo Pratt as Caroline's killer after being pressured by the LAPD.

I recognized the old cop ploy immediately. I have used it myself. You show a confused witness a photograph of the person you want in jail and, nine times out of ten, if you press hard enough, the witness will say what you want to hear. After more than three years, Mr. Olsen had suddenly become clairvoyant enough to tell the LAPD that Geronimo Pratt was the one who had shot Caroline Olsen.

Then Dred Scott dropped the clincher. Scott said, "The LAPD won't tell the jury that Olsen positively identified at least three other suspects before he identified Pratt."

Scott continued. He told how the Los Angeles Police Department had recovered a weapon from John Huggins' house after the UCLA murders. He said that the LAPD ballistics expert would testify that the weapon found in Huggins' house belonged to Pratt and that it was the gun that was used to kill Caroline Olsen, even though the barrel was missing.

I knew enough about ballistics to know that you had to compare rifling marks on a round of ammunition as it slammed out of the barrel of a gun with the rifling in the gun barrel to prove that the round that killed a certain person had come from the gun in question. The Los Angeles Police Department did not follow that procedure and they did not tell the jury so.

Scott gave us a rundown on Julius Carl Butler, the prime witness against Pratt, who had been an informer for the Los Angeles Police Department and the FBI for several years. Scott said Pratt had expelled Butler from the Black Panther Party because Butler was a violent person. Julius Butler was no longer effective as an informer, so Butler decided to get even with Pratt by claiming that Pratt had confessed to Butler to having killed Caroline Olsen.

Dred Scott said, "We will close our informant file on Butler during the trial so that Butler can say he is not an FBI informant."

I looked around the room. Scott and some of the agents were smiling. Two other agents winked at each other.

Scott said, "It took some doing, but it looks as though we have Pratt cold this time."

I thought to myself that Pratt would not be convicted if the Black Panther attorney in San Francisco, Charles R. Garry, represented Pratt. The trial started and I did not give it a second thought because I believed in our system of justice. I thought that an innocent person could not be convicted in a court of law in these United States. I had lost cases against guilty persons. How could an innocent person go to jail? I learned later that I still had been naive. Elmer "Geronimo" Pratt was convicted in Los Angeles Superior Court and sentenced to life in prison.

My supervisor and several agents on the racial squad knew that Pratt was innocent because the FBI had wiretap logs proving that Pratt was in the San Francisco area several hours before the shooting of Caroline Olsen and that he was there the day after the murder.

The Los Angeles office had had a wiretap on Panther headquarters in Los Angeles for a two-week period covering the date of December 18, 1968. These wiretap logs could prove that Elmer Pratt was in the San Francisco area on the day Caroline Olsen was shot to death.

I reviewed the Black Panther Party file that showed that the Los Angeles FBI office had had a wiretap on the Panther office at 4115 South Central Avenue from November 15, 1968 through 2:00 P.M., December 20, 1968. In other cases for which I had reviewed wiretaps, such as on radical attorneys such as Charles R. Garry and William Kunstler, I simply asked the clerk who handled the "JUNE" files—the records pertaining to wiretaps and other electronic surveillances—for the records and telephone logs. I had worked with wiretap information since 1952, and this was the first time in my twenty-five-year career that I could not find the Panther wiretap logs for the period November 15 through December 20, 1968. Someone had destroyed these logs so there would be no proof that Elmer Pratt had been in the San Francisco area on December 18, 1968.

A wiretap by the San Francisco FBI office on Panther headquarters placed Pratt in the Bay area just hours before the shooting. An illegal wiretap in Oakland, which was paid for by the FBI from a bogus informant file under the name of Ozzie Penz, possibly a code name for the Oakland Police, placed Pratt in Oakland the day after the murder.

This is a total of three wiretaps known to the FBI with information that placed Pratt in the San Francisco area before, during, and after the murder of Caroline Olsen, and yet the FBI withheld this information from the court and the jury.

When Julius Carl Butler testified under oath in the Pratt trial, he said he had not been an informer for the police or the FBI. I reviewed Butler's FBI informant file, number 170-1259. The file shows that FBI agents, including Richard Wallace Held, who retired as Special Agent in Charge of the San Francisco FBI office in 1993, had been in contact with Butler for more than two years before the Pratt trial and that an FD-209 Informant Contact form had been filled out more than two dozen times. The Butler informant file was opened on a memo from agent Richard Wallace Held dated July 9, 1970. Butler was contacted by the FBI at least once a month for a two-year period. The Butler informant file was closed before the trial started and it was re-opened after Elmer Pratt was convicted. Both Butler and the FBI deny that Butler was an informant, but the informant file has now been made available to Pratt's attorneys, and it is there for anyone to review. The information on Butler's status as an informer for the LAPD and the FBI is now a matter of public record in the courts, but Pratt is still serving time. The FBI did not tell the court or the jury that Elmer Pratt also had been a target of COINTELPRO to be neutralized.

Pratt was not the only case of FBI-orchestrated miscarriages of justice that I learned about.

Sometime later, I attended a special seminar at the FBI's National Academy at Quantico, Virginia. Friends from other offices were there, as was *Gregg York,* a long-time friend from Chicago. York and I had conducted nearly 100 bag jobs together in Chicago and we came to trust each other with our jobs and our lives. We shared some of the FBI's darkest secrets.

There is a lounge at the FBI National Academy which sells low-alcohol beer in the evening after classes, but no hard liquor. Gregg York and I had finished a few pitchers of beer one night as we discussed old times. I don't recall just how the subject of the Black Panther Party came up. I may have started the conversation by comparing the work on the Los Angeles racial squad to the bag jobs Gregg and I had done in Chicago.

I told York that some agents in Los Angeles had informants who had assassinated Black Panther members and I told him how Geronimo Pratt had been framed for murder and had been sentenced to life in prison.

York grinned and said he had a better story than that.

York told me about the December 1969 raid on the Chicago Panther headquarters in which Fred Hampton and Mark Clark had been killed by the Chicago police. He said the FBI had arranged for the raid by telling the police that the Panthers had numerous guns and explosives, and that they would shoot any police officer who entered the building.

As York outlined the details of what had happened during the pre-dawn raid on December 4, 1969, directed by the state attorney general's office, his smile went away. His mouth tightened. York looked as though he was about to confess to a horrible sin. We had been through some tough times together and I admired him as a friend and fellow agent. York had always been there when we needed him on a difficult bag job. He was one of the best agents with whom I had ever worked. From his expression I felt he was about to tell me something I did not want to hear and something he should not tell me. York looked over his shoulder in both directions, to be sure no one was listening. We were alone at a corner table. I poured another glass of beer and sipped it while York told his story.

York explained that agent Roy Mitchell had an informant in the Chicago Black Panther Party and that the informant had given Mitchell a detailed floor plan of Panther headquarters along with a description of their weapons cache. He explained that the Chicago FBI office had held a conference with the Chicago police and had detailed the violent background of the Panthers and their collection of firearms. He said, "We gave them a copy of the detailed floor plan from Mitchell's informant so that they could raid the place and kill the whole lot."

I was speechless. Gregg York had just confessed to me his part, as a supervisor in the Chicago office, in the FBI's plot to assassinate the Panthers in a style similar to the Chicago gangland murders of the 1950s. York had confessed to being an accessory to murder. The judge later ruled that indeed there had been a conspiracy between the FBI and the police in this case.

We did not speak for what seemed a long time. I kept thinking of how my old friend thought I was on his side when it came to killing African Americans. I felt sorry for Gregg York because he was still fighting Hoover's imaginary enemies: the communists, the Native Americans and the African Americans.

We began to talk again, and York said, "We expected about twenty Panthers to be in the apartment when the police raided the place. Only two of those black nigger fuckers were killed, Fred Hampton and Mark Clark."

I could not take anymore of York's depraved attitude. I changed the subject to our upcoming retirements.

On the last day of the seminar I said good-bye to York and wished him well in his retirement. I never spoke to him again. During my career I had done many things that I was not proud of, but I never had been involved in a plot to murder or assassinate anyone. I knew it would be hard for me to live down the transgressions I had committed against the Constitution in what I thought were honorable acts in the defense of our country, but I had no idea how Gregg York and the other agents involved in plots to assassinate and murder innocent citizens could ever have a peaceful night's sleep.

Chapter 10

No Weathermen Anymore

I returned to the Weatherman squad on August 13, 1973. William A. Sullivan, the new Assistant Director in Charge of the Los Angeles office, which was a newly created position that Bill Nolan had hoped Wesley G. Grapp would get before retiring, said he did not see why we had to have a Weatherman squad in Los Angeles since, according to him, there were no Weathermen anymore.

It was as if Bernardine Dohrn had heard what Sullivan said, because in May 1974 the Weathermen bombed the Los Angeles offices of Evelle Younger, the attorney general of California, in retaliation for the murder of six Symbionese Liberation Army members killed in a Los Angeles Police shoot-out when the house they were in burned to the ground.

In June 1974, the Weatherman Underground bombed Gulf Oil's headquarters in Pittsburgh, Pennsylvania. In July, the Weatherman Underground Organization published a 156-page political statement titled "Prairie Fire."

On October 21, 1974, Sullivan held a closed-door conference in his plush 17th-floor office with me and James Startzel, the new Special Agent in Charge of the Security Division, and Tom Kerr, the supervisor. Sullivan was getting a lot of heat from new FBI Director Clarence M. Kelley for not catching the Weathermen fugitives.

Startzel and Kerr reeled off the usual gobbledygook about how difficult it was to locate the Weatherman fugitives with PhDs.

The problem was not that the Weathermen had college degrees, but that the majority of agents in charge and supervisors had no experience in locating and apprehending fugitives. It was much like the blind leading the blind.

Sullivan attacked Kerr personally. He accused Kerr of goofing off, of being an alcoholic, and of sleeping with his secretary. Sullivan said, "I've had reports that you smell like a brewery at eight o'clock in the morning."

Watching and listening to Kerr respond to Sullivan's charges was more embarrassing than watching Richard Nixon in his final good-bye speech. Startzel had nothing to say, and he retired nine months later. Sullivan bounced Kerr from the Weatherman squad that same day. Kerr retired one year later.

Kerr's replacement, *Ralph Lord,* was also incompetent. We had a twenty-four-hour surveillance set up on a house in Santa Monica where we thought a Weatherman had once resided. Lord instructed me to rent an apartment across the street from the house to be surveilled. The plan was for two agents to stay in the furnished apartment, which had a swimming pool, for twenty-four hours, to observe and photograph the individuals entering and leaving the house, and then be relieved by two other agents who watched and waited for another twenty-four hours. During the daylight hours there was supposed to be an outside surveillance team of two agents who surveilled unknown visitors long enough to identify them through a license plate number or street address.

When I reported to Ralph Lord that some agents were taking law courses, playing golf, sunbathing by the pool, and working on their rental properties during the day, when they were supposed to be on the twenty-four-hour surveillance, and then they submitted fraudulent surveillance logs, Lord said, "Well, things have to change." Lord made no changes and he did not speak to any of the agents about not being on duty at the apartment. Lord's incompetence was recognized by the Los Angeles office and he was soon promoted to FBI headquarters in Washington, D.C. The six-month Santa Monica surveillance was a complete waste of the taxpayers' money.

The last bag job of which I had knowledge took place in 1975. *Daniel Parker,* owner of a Hollywood sound-dubbing studio, called the Los Angeles FBI office on May 10, 1975, to report that Emile de Antonio, a radical filmmaker, was using his studio to edit a movie.

Parker claimed that he accidentally had overheard parts of the sound track on his master console. Parker said he had heard Bernadine Dohrn and other members of the Weatherman Underground Organization talking about bombing the U.S. Capitol building in February 1971. He also had overheard Cathy Wilkerson and Kathy Boudin, both Weatherman fugitives, talking about their escape from the townhouse explosion in Greenwich Village on March 6, 1970, which had killed Diana Oughton, Ted Gold, and Terry Robins.

What Daniel Parker had heard was part of the sound track from the movie de Antonio had made, with these fugitives, about the Weatherman Underground Organization. Parker made a copy of the sound track, violating copyright laws, and turned it over to the FBI.

The bureau supervisor at FBI headquarters wanted the film itself. Emile de Antonio had eluded the poorly run surveillances directed by our new and totally incompetent supervisor, *Jauf Medina.*

Several FBI agents in New York City broke into Emile de Antonio's apartment without a search warrant looking for the Weathermen movie, but they found nothing.

On May 21, 1975, Medina called Assistant U.S. Attorney Bonner to have subpoenas issued for Haskel Wexler, the cinematographer for the movie, who also filmed "One Flew Over the Cuckoo's Nest"; Emile de Antonio; Mrs. de Antonio; Mary Lampson, de Antonio's assistant; and Jeffrey Wexler.

I told Jauf Medina that de Antonio was exempt from any subpoena issued by the U.S. Attorney in Los Angeles because only the U.S. Attorney General can authorize subpoenas for a member of the news media.

The next day the Los Angeles office received urgent teletypes from the Chicago, New York, and Portland FBI offices. They all disagreed with the subpoenas. Chicago wrote: "The film is a documentary, therefore it is covered under the privilege of Freedom of the Press." New York wrote: "Subpoenas are often self-defeating." Portland wrote: "The movie presents an excellent opportunity to apprehend the [Weatherman fugitives.] Subpoenas would destroy that chance."

On June 6, 1975, a press conference was held in Los Angeles by de Antonio's attorney opposing the subpoenas. Hollywood film celebrities and other supporters had rallied to the film's defense. The publicity captured the attention of Attorney General Edward H. Levi, who immediately quashed the subpoenas.

Haskel Wexler had borrowed a car from Gerald Feil, a friend of Wexler's, to film some Weatherman movie scenes at the Martin Luther King, Jr. Hospital in Los Angeles. After the fiasco with the subpoenas, Medina wanted to kidnap Gerald Feil.

Medina said, "We'll get a hold of Feil, put him in a bureau car, and back it up to the edge of a cliff. We'll sweat that son of a bitch until he tells the truth."

I had no idea what information Feil might have about the movie. As far as we could tell, Feil had loaned his car to Wexler and knew nothing about the movie. I knew that Medina had lost face and had taken leave of his senses after Levi had quashed the subpoenas. So, now he wanted to show the agents on the Weatherman squad and the agents in the other field offices that he had the ability to catch the ever-elusive Weathermen who had had the effrontery to make a movie on the streets of Los Angeles right under his nose.

The surveillances led by Medina were the sloppiest I had ever witnessed in my twenty-five-year career. If we agents in Chicago had operated such sloppy surveillances against the Communist Party in the 1950s as Medina had led in 1975, all of us would have been dismissed with prejudice. As it was, Medina was promoted to the bureau in Washington, D.C.

One surveillance team on Emile de Antonio left a surveillance schedule on the front seat of a surveillance car in Venice. A passerby saw the schedule with Haskel Wexler's name listed and called Wexler to tell him of the FBI surveillance.

Medina ran another surveillance in Santa Barbara on a National Lawyers Guild attorney, Richard A. Frishman. Mr. Frishman is a member of the California Attorneys for Criminal Justice, a group co-founded by Charles R. Garry.

Medina had sent me to work with three of the long-hair "beards"* on the Frishman surveillance. I did not know that *Bob Lark* and *Ray Doe* had two waitresses with them on the Saturday night surveillance. Not only were these waitresses privy to a top secret FBI sur-

---

* The term "beards" was used for FBI agents who had grown beards and shoulder length hair to go undercover.

veillance of an attorney, but they stayed in Santa Barbara for the weekend. Who knows what other FBI secrets the two waitresses gleaned from the undercover FBI agents?

I was shocked to hear one of the waitresses speak over the FBI car radio. She said, "Frishman made a right turn on De La Vina."

Tim House, who was also on the Frishman surveillance that weekend, said, "All the beards are fucking them."

I immediately turned off my radio and went back to my motel. When I reported this outrageous violation of bureau rules and breach of FBI security to Medina, he did nothing.

Chapter   11

Lying to the GAO

The General Accounting Office, also known as the GAO, began the first-ever audit of FBI files in 1974. The GAO reviewed FBI files pursuant to a request by the honorable Peter W. Rodino, Jr., chairman of the Committee on the Judiciary in the U.S. House of Representatives.

The GAO thought that the review would be from a random sampling of files, but the FBI refused them access to the files and then selected the files shown to the GAO. This is what we in the FBI called "selective random sampling."

The GAO reviewed the FBI's "Manual of Instructions" and the "Manual of Rules and Regulations," finding that "a sound basis exists for opening an investigation, for achieving investigative results, and for reporting to headquarters."

The FBI told the GAO that it had instituted internal security* investigations because of violations of various laws. To convince the GAO that this was true, agents showed the GAO files that contained information indicating that there had been a referral for prosecution, either federal or local, and that there had been a prosecution and a conviction. Of the 17,528 cases investigated by the ten FBI offices that were audited, only 533 cases were referred for prosecution. The conviction rate was a terrible 1.3%.

---

* An internal security investigation is one that is conducted by the FBI when information is received concerning the security of the United States within its geographical boundaries. The Central Intelligence Agency (CIA) conducts security investigations outside the United States.

The GAO concluded from their audit of FBI files that the FBI's statistics were questionable, the investigations were passive, and that the FBI had not adequately examined procedures for maintaining security data. Even though the GAO operated in the FBI's thick cloud of obfuscation, it had exposed the FBI's incompetence.

From September 1973 to September 1974 the racial squad opened 1,800 phony cases on computerized lists stolen from organizations under investigation. I worked on some cases opened from a computerized list of names lifted from a bag job on the American Nazi Party. The racial squad never figured out what the list of names meant, but we investigated nearly 2,000 individuals on that list, and some agents wrote reports to Washington claiming that these people were members of the American Nazi Party, when actually we did not know whether the list represented individuals who had bought a new car or had bought a magazine subscription.

This is significant because those innocent individuals, who were recklessly reported as being members of the American Nazi Party by some incompetent FBI agent using an unidentified mailing list, will never be able to obtain a job with the U.S. or any state government, and they will never know why they were rejected for employment unless they request their file under the Freedom of Information Act.

During that period the FBI opened cases on several thousand telephone numbers called by members of the Black Panther Party, including business establishments and public institutions, much the same way as I was ordered to do on the Weathermen in 1970.

The FBI opened 129 cases based on the names from an address book taken from a black man who had been arrested by the LAPD on local charges.

The FBI opened twenty-six fake cases from license numbers taken from cars parked near the area where a memorial was held on August 7, 1973, in remembrance of the martyrdom of Jonathan Jackson.

The GAO reported in 1976, after operating in the FBI's debilitating smoke screen, that "investigations of the Klan and the American Indian Movement are least extensive. Only leaders, activists, and persons in attendance when illegal acts were committed or planned are subject to full-scale investigations. Members or supporters are not subjected to preliminary inquiries to determine their propensities for violence."

In contrast to what the GAO was told, the FBI had conducted a full-field investigation of every member of the Los Angeles chapter of the American Indian Movement based on copies of membership applications that were surreptitiously removed from the movement office in Los Angeles by an FBI informant. Because the FBI had a quota of five informants for every agent, many AIM members became fake informants, unbeknown to the AIM member.

The FBI responded to the 1976 GAO report by announcing that it had changed from the Hoover era of "quantity" statistics to the new program under Director Clarence Kelley of "quality" cases.

Neither the FBI nor Clarence Kelley explained publicly, or to the agents, what they meant by "quality" cases. I certainly did not understand their double-talk, nor did I see a switch to quality cases. I was still working the same old phony cases when I retired a year after the GAO report was released. If the FBI had had a notion to work quality cases, it would have had to dismiss half its agents, because 90% of the cases in the Security Division were fabricated.

The FBI did not reduce the staff in Los Angeles and it did not cut back on the request for additional agents. The fact is that the office went from one Special Agent in Charge and one Assistant Special Agent in Charge, to a top-heavy administration of one Assistant Director in Charge and three Special Agents in Charge, one each for the Administrative Division, the Criminal Division, and the Security Division. This was after the FBI had gone from "quantity" statistical cases to "quality" investigations. The Los Angeles office was drowning in over-supervision.

On August 14, 1980, the GAO issued another report on the FBI's "quality" investigations. It stated that 49% of the sampled cases had not involved any federal violation. Accepting the fiscal year 1979 statistics at face value, 22% of agent investigative time was not being spent on top-quality cases, and 50% of the "quality" cases were declined by the various U.S. Attorneys because no federal jurisdiction existed. In sixty-nine of the seventy-six sampled cases, the FBI guidelines had not been followed.

The GAO found that the FBI had spent time on ninety-nine cases which resulted in no federal prosecution. In the FBI's new "quality system," GAO found that 30% of the closed cases had not been prosecutable because of the FBI's inability to identify a subject or gather sufficient evidence for prosecution.

In 1974, Dred Scott supervised the agents who reviewed the files before they were released to the GAO. FBI Director Clarence Kelley gave Dred Scott a cash incentive award of $500 for outstanding devotion to duty—in other words, indirectly for the obfuscation of the GAO during the file review.

Chapter 12

Perjury Before Congress

Fourteen years after ex-FBI agent William W. Turner requested a congressional investigation of Hoover's FBI, Congress responded. In 1975, the Church Committee* began questioning top FBI officials under oath about the FBI's past intelligence gathering techniques.

Some of those who testified are as follows:

James B. Adams, Assistant to the Director-Deputy Associate Director
W. Raymond Wannall, Assistant Director, Intelligence Division
Joseph G. Deegan, Section Chief, Extremist Investigations
Edward P. Grigalus, Unit Chief, Subversive Informants

Soon after Raymond Wannall testified before Congress, he traveled to Los Angeles, where he held a briefing for agents in the Security Division of the Los Angeles FBI field office, which I attended. Wannall explained how he and other top FBI officials had conspired to alter testimony before the Church Committee.

Mr. Wannall said, "When it came to [testifying about] black bag jobs, we selected agents who had no firsthand knowledge of illegal break-ins to conduct a search of the [FBI] files." He said that those agents who had had no experience in bag jobs would not know where to look for information on bag jobs. Wannall said that

---

* The Church Committee refers to the Select Committee To Study Governmental Operations With Respect To Intelligence Activities of the U.S. Senate formed in 1975 and under the direction of Senator Frank Church.

the only documentation they could find was what existed in the indices for surreptitious entries, which was not much. Wannall said that no effort was made to interview agents who, based on information in their personnel files, might have had any knowledge of bag jobs. Wannall said, "We did a good job of concealing the extent of black bag jobs."

James B. Adams also lied about the number of illegal mail-opening projects done by the FBI. Some mail openings were mentioned to appease Congress. Adams had inspected the Chicago office in 1959 when another squad had an ongoing project to illegally open mail at the U.S. Post Office. I often arrived in the FBI office around 5:00 A.M. to gather equipment for another black bag job, only to see special agents *Jack Calibre, John Redman, Sean Conley,* and *Merv Sanders* preparing their Speed Graphic cameras and letter-opening equipment in the squad room area. I once asked Jack and John what they were doing. John replied, "We open mail at the post office before the carriers arrive to sort it. We photograph letters with good information and then reseal the letters and send them on their way."

Adams knew about the mail openings, but he did not tell Congress about them.* James Z. Dick, a Washington attorney who was staff counsel to the Church Committee, told a *Chicago Tribune* reporter in 1986 that he could not recall ever having been told of any FBI mail-opening program in Chicago. James Dick said that the FBI would have been in contempt of Congress if it had, in fact, failed to turn over information about mail openings in Chicago.

Edward P. Grigalus, who was present during Adams' and Wannall's testimony before the Church Committee, was the relief supervisor for Joseph P. McMahan, Chicago's Security Coordinator, during 1952-1953 when I helped perform black bag jobs on Leon Katzen and other suspected Communist Party members. Grigalus knew about the bag jobs in Chicago but he said nothing to Congress about them.

---

* He also knew about the bag jobs because he had reviewed my file prior to his interview with me in 1959.

By 1971, Congress had repealed the Emergency Detention Act. The FBI told Congress that it had destroyed the Security Index—another lie. I saw over 5,000 Security Index cards in Los Angeles. When the Administrative Index, known as the ADEX, was created in 1972, many names on the former Security Index were transferred to the ADEX. The remaining Security Index cards were stamped "Canceled" and moved to a different file drawer. The cards were not "destroyed," as the FBI had led Congress to believe.

During the ADEX revision process in 1972, Bill Nolan ordered me to move an eighty-year-old woman's name from the Security Index to the ADEX because the woman had gone to a Fourth of July picnic sponsored by the Communist Party that year. Disgusted, I destroyed the file memorandum showing that the woman had attended the picnic and contributed $5 to the Communist Party. I submitted a memorandum deleting the woman's name from the old Security Index and the new ADEX.

Adams told Congress in 1975 that the ADEX "is a very small list, relatively small. It involves approximately 1,250 names at the present time." At that time, in fact, Los Angeles had 3,959 canceled Security Index cards in a drawer next to the ADEX cards. Names such as Jane Fonda and Thomas Hayden, founder of the Students for a Democratic Society, had been removed from the ADEX just days before Adams testified so that Adams could deceive Congress.

Raymond Wannall gave me the impression that he was proud of the fact that he, Adams, and the other co-conspirators had perjured themselves before the Church Committee.

I was furious with Adams, Grigalus, and Wannall for lying to Congress about the bag jobs that other agents and I had done in the 1950s, believing that we were defending our country. The FBI should have told Congress, "Yes, we did illegal break-ins against enemies of this country in an effort to preserve the Constitution. If we did wrong, we are sorry. But remember, gentlemen, that this country is safe from communism, the Weathermen, and many other groups that wish to overthrow this great country by force and violence." I think Congress would have agreed that we acted in the best interests of the citizens of the United States in that time period. By lying to Congress, the FBI officials admitted that what other agents and I had done to preserve freedom in America was absolutely wrong and that they were ashamed to admit to the wrongdoing. I knew then that the whole security intelligence operation of the FBI was no better than Adolph Hitler's Gestapo. The only difference was that the Gestapo did not pretend to be the good guys in white hats. The Gestapo wore black, and they were proud.

In 1975, the Socialist Workers Party sued the FBI for the illegal investigative techniques used against them over the years. The FBI argued that the exposure of informants would devastate the FBI's informant program. I reviewed the informant files in 1976, and know that the FBI's stance was an absolute lie. The only devastation the FBI informant program would suffer if the truth were known would be the fact that most FBI informers were paper informers.

When I read the nonsense FBI argument in the communiqués from the Los Angeles office to FBI headquarters, I wanted to puke. I knew that agent *Stan Hunlast* had compiled the phony statistics about exposure of FBI informers. He was one of the greatest offenders of the FBI informant quota system that I have ever known. Hunlast received a $500 bonus for developing more informers than any other agent in the Los Angeles office while I was on the racial squad from 1972 to 1973. I know his informers were bogus because he gave me one when I was under the office quota, and another of his phony informants reported on a Brown Beret meeting that never took place. Another agent and I had suspected Hunlast of operating bogus informants, so we gave him details of a phony meeting, and a few days later Hunlast submitted an informant report on the fake Brown Beret meeting.

Adams told Judge Thomas Griesa during the Socialist Workers Party lawsuit that the FBI promised informers confidentiality. This is not true. The main purpose behind developing informers is to prepare them as witnesses in a court case. The informant's file even had a comment to be checked off showing that the informer had been told that she or he might be called as a witness.

Chapter 13

COINTELPRO

The FBI's Secret War on Political Freedom

In early November 1976, I went for my annual physical examination at the medical center in San Pedro, California. A relatively new doctor discovered that I had a double hernia in the lower abdomen.

I underwent surgery after Thanksgiving, and took a week of sick leave to recover. Since driving a car was the most painful movement for me, I stayed on our sailboat and kept myself busy crafting a compartment for three five-gallon propane tanks for long-distance cruising.

I returned to work in December and was relieved of many of my investigative cases because of my condition. In January 1977, I was assigned the task of reviewing files for the numerous Freedom of Information Act (FOIA) requests that were flooding the FBI. The majority of the FOIA requests assigned to me were related to the Black Panther Party and Friends of the Black Panthers. During my career I had heard rumors of many of the COINTELPRO tricks that the FBI had used to neutralize persons that Hoover and the FBI did not like. For the last five months of my career I had the opportunity to review the files of the Los Angeles FBI office and see for myself just how far some agents had gone to disrupt or ruin the lives of decent individuals.

COINTELPRO is the FBI code word for an unconscionable program that was officially in operation and documented on paper from August 1956 to April 1971. The program is still in operation today, but under a different code name. The operation is no longer placed on paper where it can be discovered through the release of documents under the Freedom of Information Act.

COINTELPRO, taken from the words counter*intel*ligence *pro*-gram, is the FBI's program to thwart the efforts of any organization or person they think is unacceptable. The stated purpose of COIN-TELPRO is to expose, disrupt, misdirect, discredit, or otherwise neutralize the activities of the various subversive organizations and their members and individuals whom FBI officials categorize as op-posed to the national interests. The FBI made no distinction be-tween the threats posed by the Soviet Union, by the communists within the United States, or by political and environmental activists.

The FBI collected massive volumes of information on lawful groups and law-abiding citizens, whether they associated with commu-nists, socialists, the American Civil Liberties Union, Native Ameri-cans, the National Association for the Advancement of Colored People, or Hollywood actors, directors, and writers, who voiced their right to political freedom. Any individual who expressed an opinion against the House Committee on Un-American Activities, no matter how private that person believed his or her thoughts and words were, became a target of the FBI. Present-day environmental activists are tar-geted by the FBI, according to news reports.

The domestic intelligence programs of the FBI were estab-lished under presidential authority before World War II. The FBI let Congress believe that much of the domestic intelligence activity ended after World War II. It did not.

A clear example of the FBI's continued COINTELPRO is in the FBI's alleged involvement in the 1990 bombing of the vehicle occupied by Judy Bari and Darryl Cherney. Both Bari and Cherney are key organizing members of the radical environmental organiza-tion Earth First! and were on their way to an important organizing meeting when their car exploded, leaving Bari confined to a wheel-chair. A congressional probe is underway concerning the FBI's pos-sible involvement in the bombing, which was an effort by the FBI to neutralize Judy Bari. The case is currently in the courts.

When I was the case agent on at least two dozen leaders of the Communist Party in Chicago in the 1950s, Hoover said that it was my responsibility to call to the attention of the counterintelligence

coordinator suggestions and possibilities for implementing COIN-
TELPRO. I was told not to discuss COINTELPRO with anyone outside the FBI, including my wife or relatives. I never mentioned a
word to anyone. My approach to COINTELPRO in the 1950s was
to let individuals keep their jobs so that I could keep track of where
they worked. I had no personal vendetta against the communists, but
I did want to know how to find them just in case they tried to overthrow my country by force and violence, as Hoover said they might.
In that case, they would have had to deal with me and there would
have been no holds barred.

The FBI targeted the following persons for COINTELPRO:

1. Professors, teachers, and educators.
2. Labor union organizers or leaders.
3. Writers, lecturers, newsmen, and entertainers.
4. Other leaders in the mass media field.
5. Doctors, lawyers, and scientists.

These organizations became COINTELPRO targets in the following years:

1. The Communist Party of the United States, 1956.
2. Socialist Workers Party, 1961.
3. White hate groups, 1964.
4. Ku Klux Klan, 1964.
5. Black Nationalist hate groups, 1967.
6. New Left, 1968.

Many of the organizations were clearly defined groups except
for those of the New Left.

Neither Hoover nor his associates at FBI headquarters ever defined the New Left. The only definition I ever heard was that the
New Left was newer than the Old Left. The Old Left referred to the
old communists and socialists.

Anyone who was an activist after about 1965, even if they
were only students protesting a college dean or some college program they did not like, were shoveled into the New Left. Even high
school students smoking marijuana or wearing clothes which

Hoover's G-men thought were outrageous were considered a part of the New Left and were targets of the FBI's COINTELPRO.

The activists calling for an end to the Vietnam war were dumped into the New Left. Activists who alleged police brutality or made scurrilous attacks against J. Edgar Hoover and the bureau in an attempt to get the FBI off college campuses were logged into the New Left. Native Americans and African Americans who sought equal rights under the law became the New Left and COINTELPRO targets. Legitimate and nonviolent protesters, no matter what the cause, were targeted because they were lending aid and comfort to the more disruptive groups.

One file I reviewed in 1977 had a letter from Hoover to the Los Angeles office dated August 9, 1968. Hoover had authorized the mailing of a letter under the fictitious organizational name, "Black Nationalists for Freedom," aimed at New Left groups. Hoover had edited the letter to read, "If you don't know it man, the head whitey of the Communist Party in the United States told newsmen in San Francisco the SDS was one of the Party's soul brothers."

Another file revealed a COINTELPRO attack authorized on September 23, 1968, against the *Los Angeles Free Press* and *Open City*, two underground newspapers in the Los Angeles area. The purpose of the attack was to drive both papers out of business because they carried articles against the U.S. government and the business establishment.

In a letter to Hoover dated March 7, 1969, the Los Angeles FBI office announced that it had been successful in closing down the newspaper *Open City*. *Open City* ceased publication only ten weeks short of its second birthday.

I was disturbed to see this information because I had the impression that this country believed in freedom of the press. I was beginning to believe the statements by critics that Hoover and the FBI had a police state mentality.

I reviewed another file showing that the Los Angeles FBI office had engaged in COINTELPRO activities against local colleges and high schools. The Los Angeles office had mailed anonymous letters to the parents of students telling the parents about the sexual activities of the members of the Students for a Democratic Society at colleges their daughters attended.

After the parents of college students had been mailed the anonymous letters, the Los Angeles office mailed anonymous letters to parents of daughters in fifty-two high schools in the surrounding area. J. Edgar Hoover had approved of the mailing on February 7, 1969. An official of the city of Los Angeles, who was a retired FBI agent, assisted in this COINTELPRO operation. The schools whose students' parents received the COINTELPRO letters were:

William Tell Aggeley High School, Chatsworth
Banning High School, Wilmington
Bell High School, Bell
Belmont High School, Los Angeles
Birmingham High School, Van Nuys
Canoga Park High School, Canoga Park
Carson High School, Torrence
Chatsworth High School, Chatsworth
Grover Cleveland High School, Reseda
James F. Cooper High School, San Pedro
Dorsey High School, Los Angeles
Eagle Rock High School, Los Angeles
Fairfax High School, Los Angeles
Francis Polytechnic High School, Sun Valley
Benjamin Franklin High School, Los Angeles
John C. Fremont High School, Los Angeles
Golden Gate High School, Los Angeles
Gardena High School, Gardena
James A. Garfield High School, Los Angeles
Granada Hills High School, Granada Hills
Ulysses S. Grant High School, Van Nuys
Alexander Hamilton High School, Los Angeles
Hollywood High School, Los Angeles
Huntington Park High School, Huntington Park
Andrew Jackson High School, Los Angeles
Thomas Jefferson High School, Los Angeles
David Jordan High School, Los Angeles
Abraham Lincoln High School, Los Angeles

Los Angeles High School, Los Angeles
Manual Arts High School, Los Angeles
John Marshall High School, Los Angeles
Metropolitan High School, Los Angeles
James Monroe High School, Sepulveda
Narbonne High School, Harbor City
North Hollywood High School, North Hollywood
Palisades High School, Pacific Palisades
Ramona High School, Los Angeles
Reseda High School, Reseda
Roosevelt High School, Los Angeles
Betsy Ross High School, Los Angeles
San Fernando High School, San Fernando
San Pedro High School, San Pedro
South Gate High School, South Gate
Sylmar High School, Sylmar
William H. Taft High School, Woodland Hills
University High School, Los Angeles
Van Nuys High School, Van Nuys
Venice High School, Los Angeles
Verdugo Hills High School, Tujunga
George Washington High School, Los Angeles
Westchester High School, Los Angeles
Woodrow Wilson High School, Los Angeles

After seeing the COINTELPRO letters to parents of college and high school students, I knew that the FBI had gone off the deep end and had become a secret police state. I did not know the extent to which J. Edgar Hoover and his agents had gone to control the average citizen's mind, thoughts, and actions until I had read the files. Very few citizens know the extent to which the FBI has gone to control our society. The FBI thinks it knows what is best for the country.

Some individuals may think COINTELPRO is all part of the secret police game of intelligence work. It is not. It is a threat to our freedom when a police agency in a democracy takes it upon itself to be judge and jury and to decide who should be fired from a job or what newspaper should go out of business. Such a police agency walks in the shadow of Adolph Hitler's Gestapo when it decides who should be assassinated or framed for murder just to silence his or her political rhetoric. It is monstrous to know that the FBI actually wrote anonymous letters to parents of high school and college students about the sexual behavior, manner of dress, and hair styles of SDS members. It is frightening to know that the FBI is into thought control at the high school and college level. It is unknown just how far this thought control process actually reaches. It may go all the way to kindergarten.

On February 1, 1977, I reviewed the "Key Activists Album," a photograph album of the top political activists in the United States. Among the names listed were:

Actress Jane Fonda
SDS founder Thomas Hayden
Attorney William Kunstler
Michael Lerner, Assistant Professor of Philosophy, Trinity College

It is a sad state of affairs when the FBI, instead of fighting crime, has to investigate activists, lawyers, and professors. The Attorney General should see to it that a thorough house cleaning is done inside the FBI and establish controls over the FBI director and the agents to assure every citizen that the FBI is not a loose cannon running amuck in COINTELPRO.

Because I was assigned to the Panthers unit in the bureau, I have firsthand knowledge of several cases of harassment against Black Panthers and their supporters. Friends of the Panthers was an organization of white sympathizers, which included playwright Donald Freed and actress Jean Seberg. The bureau launched particularly disturbing campaigns to "neutralize" them.

A favorite FBI dirty trick was to accuse a leader of an organization of being a police informant. This is one of the tactics the FBI used against Donald Freed, who was a college professor, an award-winning playwright, and head of the Friends of the Panthers. In 1969, Freed became a general nuisance to the FBI, and to Hoover in particular, by making a scurrilous attack upon the director. Hoover regularly went ballistic when he heard of attacks against him. Freed wrote the prize-winning Broadway play "Inquest," which is about Julius and Ethel Rosenberg, who were executed in the electric chair at Sing Sing Prison in Ossining, New York, in 1953, for allegedly giving atomic bomb secrets to the Russians. "Inquest" was critical of the trial judge, Irving Kaufman, who had promised his good friend J. Edgar Hoover, even before the trial was over and before the jury had found the Rosenbergs guilty, that he would give the Rosenbergs the death penalty.

Donald Freed's play opened on Broadway in April 1969, while I was assigned to the New York City office. The *New York Times* had reviewed the play two weeks in a row, April 20 and April 27, 1969.

Judge Irving Kaufman was on the Circuit Court of Appeals, Second Circuit, in 1969. He telephoned his good buddy Hoover to complain about Donald Freed's play and the *New York Times* review.

When I heard of the incident it made me wonder about Kaufman's stability. It is one thing to dislike a playwright's point of view on a prize-winning Broadway play, but quite another for a member of the U.S. Appeals Court to call the FBI Director to request an investigation, to request a COINTELPRO, and to ask him to notify the attorney general of the United States.

A memorandum from bureau supervisor W.A. Branigan to William C. Sullivan dated May 2, 1969, captioned "JULIUS ROSENBERG, ESPIONAGE - RUSSIA," and referring to Freed's play, reflects that, "On April 29, 1969, Judge Irving Kaufman, Circuit Court of Appeals, Second Circuit, telephonically contacted the Director concerning the above-mentioned play. Judge Kaufman was alarmed that the *New York Times* reviewed this play two weeks in a row, which was highly unusual. Judge Kaufman indicated that he understands the play is critical of the Director. The Judge added that he felt the Attorney General should be notified."

On May 7, 1969, Judge Irving R. Kaufman, using stationery of the U.S. Court of Appeals, wrote a personal letter to Hoover. It reads, "Dear Edgar; Thank you so much for your letter of May 2, furnishing me with the background information of the gentleman responsible for writing the play.

With my gratitude and affection, I am, sincerely yours, Irving." (See pages 113-115 for the memo and Kaufman's letter.)

During the Church Committee hearings in 1975-1976, the FBI told Congress that Freed, in his capacity as head of an organization of

2477

UNITED STATES GOVERNMENT

Memorandum

TO : Mr. W. C. Sullivan

FROM : Mr. W. A. Branigan

SUBJECT: JULIUS ROSENBERG
ESPIONAGE - RUSSIA

DATE: May 2, 1969

1 - Mr. C. D. DeLoach
1 - Mr. T. E. Bishop
1 - Mr. W. C. Sullivan
1 - Mr. W. A. Branigan
1 - Inspector E. J. Hayes
1 - Mr. J. P. Lee

Memorandum recommends letters be forwarded to the Attorney General and to Judge Kaufman concerning a play entitled "The United States vs. Julius and Ethel Rosenberg" currently showing in Cleveland, Ohio, which is critical of the Government handling of that case.

On April 29, 1969, Judge Irving Kaufman, Circuit Court of Appeals, Second Circuit, telephonically contacted the Director concerning the above-mentioned play. Judge Kaufman was alarmed that the "New York Times" reviewed this play two weeks in a row on April 20 and 27, 1969, which was highly unusual. Judge Kaufman indicated that he understands the play is critical of the Director, the prosecutor, and Judge Kaufman who was the trial judge in the Rosenberg case. The Judge added that he felt the Attorney General should be informed, and the Director advised that he would let the Attorney General know.

This play opened in Cleveland on March 14, 1969, and is scheduled to continue until May 11, 1969. It was observed by an Agent of the Cleveland Office and he noted it assumes the innocence of the Rosenbergs and as was noted in the reviews, it is propaganda rather than drama. The author is Donald Martin Freed, (   )

The play is directed by Larry Tarrant, a graduate of the University of Wichita, employed as a play director in the Cleveland area for the past five years. No identifiable derogatory information on Tarrant or any of the actors or actresses in Cleveland, New York, or Bureau files

Enclosures - 2

1 -

A memorandum from bureau supervisor W.A. Branigan to William C. Sullivan dated May 2, 1969, captioned "JULIUS ROSENBERG, ESPIONAGE - RUSSIA" refers to Freed's play.

Memorandum to Mr. W. C. Sullivan
RE: JULIUS ROSENBERG
65-58236

ACTION:

     1. There is attached a letter to the Attorney General furnishing him with information concerning this play and its anti-Government slant.

     2. There is also attached a letter to Judge Irving Kaufman furnishing information concerning this play.

WGB

OK

United States Court of Appeals
United States Courthouse
Foley Square, New York, 10007

CHAMBERS OF
IRVING R. KAUFMAN
CIRCUIT JUDGE

May 7, 1969

Dear Edgar:

Thank you so much for your letter of May 2, furnishing me with the background information of the gentleman responsible for writing the play, "The United States v. Julius and Ethel Rosenberg."

I believe you will be interested in seeing a copy of a letter sent by former Federal Judge Simon Rifkind to The New York Times concerning their extensive reporting of this play.

With my gratitude and affection, I am

Sincerely yours,

Irving R. Kaufman
United States Circuit Judge

Enclosure

The Honorable John Edgar Hoover
Director, Federal Bureau of Investigation
United States Department of Justice
Washington, D. C. 20535

The May 7, 1969 personal letter from Judge Irving R. Kaufman to Hoover.

white Black Panther Party sympathizers called Friends of the Panthers, had been a COINTELPRO target in order to destroy the confidence between the Panthers and the Friends of the Panthers. According to a letter from the Los Angeles FBI office to Hoover, which was given to the Church Committee: "Any exposure [of Freed] will not only deny the Panthers money, but additionally, would cause other white supporters of the BPP to withdraw their support. It is felt that the Los Angeles chapter of the BPP could not operate without the financial support of white sympathizers."

The FBI did not tell Congress that Freed had become a COINTELPRO target in part because of Judge Kaufman's telephone call to Hoover. Kaufman's call was the straw that broke the camel's back.

Donald Freed had been an anthropology instructor at San Fernando Valley State College in Los Angeles. The case agent, *Phil Denny,* saw to it that Freed lost his contract in 1969. When Freed tried to get a job at California State College in Fullerton, California, in the fall of 1969, Denny sent word to the proper person in Fullerton and Donald Freed was not hired. (The last I knew, Freed was a professor at the University of California at Los Angeles.)

Two months after Kaufman's call to Hoover, Hoover authorized the San Francisco FBI office on July 1, 1969, to pass out 200 copies of a leaflet, created and printed by the Crime Records Division, in the vicinity of a Black Panther Party-sponsored national conference in Oakland, California, alleging that "Donald Freed is a PIG."

The FBI's leaflet read in part as follows: "We don't know what breed of a pig he is, but Freed is a LAPD PIG, an FBI PIG, a CIA PIG or maybe even a Sheriff PIG—but he is a pig, an informer who deals with his fellow pigs and betrays us all."

A copy of the leaflet was obtained from the FBI file on Donald Freed through the Freedom of Information Act. (See page 117.) I observed this leaflet in Donald Freed's Los Angeles FBI file during the 1977 file review as a result of Freed's FOIA request. The FBI documents pertaining to Judge Kaufman's telephone call to Hoover were also obtained through the Freedom of Information Act. These documents were given to me by Donald Freed in 1978.

The COINTELPRO against Donald Freed did not work—no harm came to him. After my retirement, I attended one of Freed's

LAW AND ORDER

DON FREED IS A
PIG

We don't know what breed of a pig
he is, but Freed is a LAPD PIG, an FBI
PIG, a CIA PIG or maybe even a Sheriff PIG
------but he is a pig, an informer who
deals with his fellow pigs and betrays us
all.

The pig as far back as 1967 appearing
at meetings of the Peace Action Council
urged acts, these acts against the
president when he visited Los Angeles in
June 1967. He said he'd lead a group to
commit acts of civil disobedience at
Century Plaza.....the PIG wasn't even
arrested.

Freed urged mass draft card burning
at the Century....the PIG never lit
a match.

Freed urged the burning of Johnson in
effigy at Century Plaza....the PIG was in
hiding.

This doesn't convince you.........especially our black brothers.....
Remember the anti-draft demonstrations in front of the draft headquarters
in Los Angeles.....everyone got arrested for blocking the entrance except
the PIG....and the PIG had urged the sitin.

Last month Freed spoke at the Huey Newton rally in front of the
federal building. Remember his chanting,"We are All Panthers, We Are All
Panthers".....and urging everyone to protect the Panthers..."with our lives
if necessary".

Shortly after this rally the PIGS struck at the heart of the Panthers
as our black brothers were arrested.

AND WHO WAS IT TALKING TO PIG FREED just ten minutes after this
rally ???????????????

All Power to the People

The leaflet created and printed by the FBI's Crime Records Division, distributed in
the vicinity of a Black Panther Party-sponsored national conference in Oakland,
California.

courses on government conspiracy at the University of Southern California. I learned why the FBI's snitch jacket did not fit. Anyone who knows Donald Freed knows he could never be a "pig" for the FBI.

Targeting Actress Jean Seberg

Jean Seberg is best known for her role in Otto Preminger's 1957 film "Saint Joan."

The FBI had monitored Seberg's checking account and found she had given over $10,000 to the Black Panther Party. Special Agent Richard Wallace Held was upset at Jean's generosity to the Panthers.

The FBI could not understand the motivation for Seberg's cash donations. I figured she was an easy touch for any hard-luck story. She constantly opened her purse to the Panthers. Other agents crassly assumed she was sexually involved with members of the Black Panther Party. Seberg was active with Friends of the Panthers.

The Los Angeles Racial Squad fired off a Confidential communiqué to Hoover about Jean Seberg stating that, "This is to furnish information that subject, a beautiful, internationally known white American actress with black extremist relationships and sympathies, is reportedly a sex pervert."

Jean Seberg was married to the world-renowned French diplomat and writer Romain Gary. They lived in an apartment on Rue du Bac in Paris. She had just returned to Paris from making a film in Durango, Mexico, in 1970.

Seberg explained to Jane Friedman, a reporter from the *International Herald Tribune,* that "she [had fallen] in love with Carlos Navarra, a Mexican 'revolutionary,' while shooting 'a bad movie named *Macho Callahan* in Durango.' Miss Seberg said Mr. Navarra was the father of the child she was expecting. 'I don't want to abort,' she said. 'Romain said he would assume fatherhood.'"

The FBI had wiretaps on the Panther headquarters in Los Angeles as well as wiretaps on the private residences of several top leaders of the Panthers in Los Angeles. Transcripts of wiretapped conversations were made available under the Freedom of Information Act. One conversation involving Seberg formed the basis of a smear campaign designed to destroy Seberg's reputation, with the goal of weakening ties between the Black Panthers and the support group Friends of the Panthers.

The call from Elaine Brown, a top leader of the Black Panther Party, placed to Seberg in Paris on April 21, 1970, is open to various interpretations. Without understanding the context of the call and the relationship between speakers, the meaning is obscured. Seberg was four months pregnant at the time.

"I'm sitting next to a friend of yours," Brown said.

Seberg asked, "Who's that? Johnny Appleseed?"

Just then Masai Hewitt, a Los Angeles Panther leader, came on the line. Seberg told him that she was going to have a baby, adding, "After not knowing and not knowing what to do about it, I'm going to go ahead, too."

"When?" asked Hewitt.

"In the fall. I'm like in the fourth month so I have a nice long wait ahead. I guess it's that year, you see."

"I guess it's all right," Hewitt replied.

"I guess, yes. I think it's all right...I'm happy about this, really..." Seberg agreed. "I ran into a thing that scared me legally about my other son. I was afraid I was going to lose custody, you know, if my former husband got wind about it and he was really very civilized and very nice about it. So it's really good, you know. So everybody you know sooner or later I guess is going to have a big tummy."

"I'm going to try not to have anything to do with it," Hewitt replied.

"Listen." Seberg said, laughing. "I'm afraid of you. You're a liar."

"I really didn't know."

"No, but I'm really happy. That's kind of the best surprise you could have. That's terrific. She told you what I call you, didn't she?"

"Yes, but I can't remember."

"Johnny Appleseed."

"No, she didn't tell me that."

"Yes, planting your little seeds around."

FBI agent Richard Wallace Held, who was then age twenty-nine and in charge of COINTELPRO against the Black Panther

Party in Los Angeles, concluded, incorrectly, that Masai Hewitt had knocked up Seberg. Seberg was teasing Hewitt, just for the fun of it. She knew the real father was Carlos Navarra, with whom she had done the movie in Mexico.

The FBI thought that since Seberg "was heavy with baby" and she had given thousands of dollars in support of the Panthers, she was ripe for plucking and "should be neutralized."

Richard Wallace Held launched another communiqué to J. Edgar Hoover requesting permission to publicize the Seberg pregnancy and to hint that Masai Hewitt just might be the father. Held thought the publication of Seberg's plight would cheapen her image with the movie-going public and be a source of embarrassment for her.

One of Hoover's fawning parasites and Panther haters at the bureau returned an answer to Los Angeles approving of the suggestion to leak the news of Seberg's pregnancy, but recommending holding off for two months until her swelling stomach "was obvious to the public, to protect the FBI wiretap on the BPP."

Richard Wallace Held thought that if he embarrassed Seberg, other Friends of the Panthers would shy away from the Panthers, thinking they too could be embarrassed.

The mood of the racist agents on the racial squad was fanatical. COINTELPRO was not the creation of an anonymous bureaucracy run amok but the calculated extension of what many racist agents considered a Hoover-authorized personal vendetta. In the view of the bureau and several agents on the racial squad, Jean Seberg was giving aid and comfort to the enemy, the Panthers. The thought of her being with a black man was unbearable for some of the agents, like Held.

I overheard *Roth Tolz* say to a group of agents, a few days after I arrived in Los Angeles from New York in May 1970, "I wonder how she'd like to gobble my dick while I shove my .38 up that black bastard's ass?" I later learned that Tolz's comment was about Jean Seberg and Masai Hewitt. I was shocked at the licentious talk about Jean Seberg and the Panthers in the squad room area, which young female clerks and stenos often frequented to carry mail and to take dictation from agents. I was used to foul language after nearly twenty years in the FBI, but the daily filthy conversation of these agents in the squad area was grossly offensive.

A Los Angeles communiqué to the director of the FBI on April 27, 1970, written by Special Agent Richard Wallace Held, requested permission to publicize the pregnancy of Jean Seberg by Raymond Masai Hewitt, Black Panther Party Minister of Education. J. Edgar Hoover approved the request, and the Los Angeles FBI office sent an anonymous letter to various Hollywood gossip columnists in Los Angeles. This document was made available by the FBI under the Freedom of Information Act from the Black Panther Party file at FBI headquarters in Washington, D.C. (See pages 122-125 for Held's letter and Hoover's response.)

The only gossip columnist known to have written an article about Jean Seberg, based on the FBI's sleazy letter, was Joyce Haber of the *Los Angeles Times*. On Tuesday, May 19, 1970, I walked into the FBI office at 11000 Wilshire Boulevard carrying a copy of the *Los Angeles Times*. The bull pen was abuzz about Dick Held's COINTELPRO letter on Jean Seberg. Joyce Haber ran the article blind to protect herself and the *Los Angeles Times* from a lawsuit, and referred to Seberg as "Miss A."

This is what the *Los Angeles Times* published on May 19, 1970:

MISS A Rates as Expectant Mother.

Let us call her Miss A, because she's the current "A" topic of chatter among the "ins" of international show-business circles. She is beautiful and blonde. Miss A came to Hollywood some years ago with the tantalizing flavor of a basket of fresh-picked berries. The critics picked at her acting debut, and in time, a handsome European picked her for his wife. After they married, Miss A lived in semi-retirement from the U.S. movie scene. But recently she burst forth as the star of a multimillion dollar musical.

Meanwhile, the outgoing Miss A was pursuing a number of free-spirited causes, among them the black revolution. She lived what she believed, which raised a few Establishment eyebrows: Not because her escorts were often blacks, but because they were black nationalists.

And now, according to all those really "in" international sources, Topic A is the baby Miss A is expecting, and its father. Papa's said to be a rather prominent Black Panther.

```
                                      F B I
                                            Date:  4/27/70

Transmit the following in _____
                                      (Type in plaintext or code)

Via ____ AIRTEL _____          REGISTERED MAIL
                                           (Priority)
```

TO: DIRECTOR, FBI (100-448006)

FROM: SAC, LOS ANGELES (157-4054) (P)

SUBJECT: COUNTERINTELLIGENCE PROGRAM
         BLACK NATIONALIST HATE GROUPS
         RACIAL INTELLIGENCE - BLACK PANTHER PARTY

Re San Francisco airtel to the Bureau dated 4/23/70, entitled, "BLACK PANTHER PARTY (BPP), LOS ANGELES DIVISION, RM-BPP."

Bureau permission is requested to publicize the pregnancy of JEAN SEBERG, well-known movie actress, by ████████████ Black Panther Party (BPP) ████████████ by advising Hollywood Gossip-Columnists in the Los Angeles area of the situation. It is felt that the possible publication of SEBERG's plight could cause her embarrassment and serve to cheapen her image with the general public.

It is proposed that the following letter from a fictitious person be sent to local columnists:

"I was just thinking about you and remembered I still owe you a favor. So--------I was in Paris last week and ran into Jean Seberg, who was heavy with baby. I thought she and Romaine had gotten

2 - Bureau (RM)
2 - San Francisco (Info) (RM) REC-51
2 - Los Angeles   100 - 447046 - 1766

RWH/fs
(6)   19 MAY 1 1970

                                     RACIAL INT. SECT.

Approved: _____   Sent _____ M Per _____
          Special Agent in Charge
                              U. S. GOVERNMENT PRINTING OFFICE 1969 O - 346-091 (2)

Communiqué to the Director of the FBI requesting permission to publicize the pregnancy of Jean Seberg by Raymond Masai Hewitt, Black Panther Party Minister of Education.

LA 157-4054

together again, but she confided the child belonged to ░░░░░░░ of the Black Panthers, one ░░░░░░░ The dear girl is getting around.

"Anyway, I thought you might get a scoop on the others. Be good and I'll see you soon..

"Love,

Sol"

Usual precautions would be taken by the Los Angeles Division to preclude identification of the Bureau as the source of the letter if approval is granted.

ROUTE IN ENVELOPE

SAC, Los Angeles (157-4054)   5/6/70
- (EC-58)
Director, FBI (100-448006) —/76 6   1 -
11.

COUNTERINTELLIGENCE PROGRAM
BLACK NATIONALIST HATE GROUPS
RACIAL INTELLIGENCE - BLACK PANTHER PARTY

Reurairtel 4/27/70.

Reairtel requests Bureau authority to forward a
letter from a fictitious person to Hollywood, California,
gossip columnists to publicize the pregnancy of Jean Seberg,
well-known white movie actress, by ▨▨▨▨▨ BPP
▨▨▨▨▨ to possibly cause her embarrassment
and tarnish her image with the general public. Information
from ▨▨▨▨ indicated that Seberg was four months
pregnant by ▨▨▨

To protect the sensitive source of information
from possible compromise and to insure the success of your
plan, Bureau feels it would be better to wait approximately
two additional months until Seberg's pregnancy would be
obvious to everyone. If deemed warranted, submit your
recommendation at that time.

1 - San Francisco

JFM:drl
(5)

NOTE:

Jean Seberg has been a financial supporter of the
BPP and should be neutralized. Her current pregnancy by
▨▨▨▨ while still married affords an opportunity for such
effort. The plan suggested by Los Angeles appears to have
merit except for the timing since the sensitive source
might be compromised if implemented prematurely. A copy is
designated to San Francisco since its sensitive source
coverage is involved.

Tolson
DeLoach
Walters
Mohr
Bishop
Casper
Callahan
Conrad
Felt
Gale
Rosen
Sullivan
Tavel
Soyars
Tele. Room
Holmes
Gandy

MAY 8 1970
MAIL ROOM ☐ TELETYPE UNIT ☐

Hoover's response to the request to start a COINTELPRO campaign against Jean
Seberg.

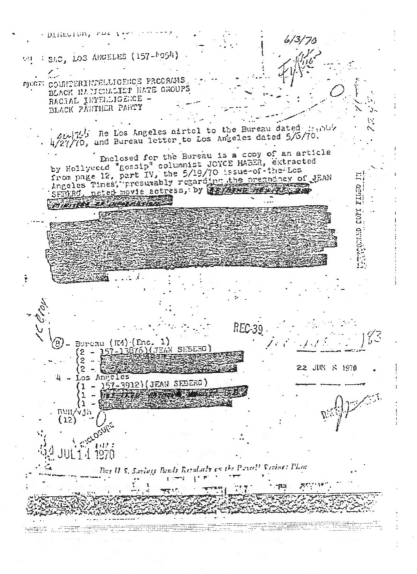

DIRECTOR, FBI

SAC, LOS ANGELES (157-4054)

SUBJECT: COUNTERINTELLIGENCE PROGRAMS
BLACK NATIONALIST HATE GROUPS
RACIAL INTELLIGENCE –
BLACK PANTHER PARTY

6/3/70

Re Los Angeles airtel to the Bureau dated
4/27/70, and Bureau letter to Los Angeles dated 5/6/70.

Enclosed for the Bureau is a copy of an article
by Hollywood "gossip" columnist JOYCE HABER, extracted
from page 12, part IV, the 5/19/70 issue of the Los
Angeles Times, presumably regarding the pregnancy of JEAN
SEBERG, noted movie actress, by ████████████████
████████████████

████████████████████████████████████
████████████████████████████████████
████████████████████████████████████
████████████████████████████████████

REC-39

8 - Bureau (RM)(Enc. 1)
(2 - 157-1376)(JEAN SEBERG)
(2 - ████████
(2 - ████████
4 - Los Angeles
(1 - 157-3912)(JEAN SEBERG)
(1 - ████████
(1 - ████████
RWH/vjh
(12)

22 JUN 8 1970

JUL 14 1970

Buy U.S. Savings Bonds Regularly on the Payroll Savings Plan

It was then that I first learned the true story behind the FBI's plan to destroy a fine actress, Jean Seberg, just because she had given money to the Black Panther Party and, according to the FBI's assumption, had slept with a black man.

On August 23, 1970, Jean Seberg gave birth by Cesarean section to a girl weighing less than four pounds. Witnesses described the baby as light-skinned with Caucasian features. With less than a 20% chance to live, she died on August 25.

In 1975, Attorney General Edward H. Levi ordered the FBI to notify all victims of COINTELPRO and to send them copies of all documents. Jean Seberg had been under tremendous emotional strain, but when she received the FBI's package of COINTELPRO documents which exposed the whole obnoxious plot to destroy her, she broke down. In late August 1979, the ninth anniversary of the birth of her deceased baby girl, Seberg left her home, taking with her a bottle of water and a tube of barbiturates. She drove to the narrow street barely two blocks long named Rue du General Appert. She wrapped herself in a blanket on the back seat. Ten days later on September 8, 1979, two policemen on motorbikes checked the car and opened the unlocked door. Fighting off nausea from the odor of decaying flesh, one officer pulled the blanket from Seberg's decomposing body. Clutched in her hand was a note addressed to her son Diego; it read simply: "Forgive me. I can no longer live with my nerves. Understand me. I know that you can and you know that I love you. Be strong. Your loving mother, Jean"

The Renault was towed away, and two sanitation workers, upset with the assignment, hosed down the street and disinfected the gutters.

After Seberg's death, Romain Gary called a press conference. The reporters thought the FBI documents were fake and that they could be the products of a writer with a great imagination. An investigation by Hebe Dorsey, a correspondent for the *International Herald-Tribune*, exposed the years of FBI cover-up. On Friday, September 14, 1979, the FBI admitted that in 1970 it had spread gossip that actress Jean Seberg had become pregnant by a member of the Black Panther Party.

William H. Webster, then FBI director, acknowledged the FBI's part in the mentally depraved and obnoxious COINTELPRO plot to neutralize Jean Seberg. Webster claimed that "the days when the FBI used derogatory information to combat advocates of unpopular causes have long since passed. We are out of that business forever."

Knowing Richard Wallace Held as I did, for a year and a half while I was on the racial squad, I don't know which achievement he holds higher in his chest of trophies, the suicide of Jean Seberg or the life imprisonment of Geronimo Pratt.

When Joyce Haber was questioned about her source for the sleazy article she did on Jean Seberg, she denied getting the information from the FBI. Haber said, "The FBI did not plant me directly because I don't know anyone in the FBI."

Seven weeks after writing to Hoover about Jean Seberg, agent Richard Wallace Held again had written to Mr. Hoover, requesting authority to send an anonymous letter to Army Archerd, a Hollywood gossip columnist for the *Daily Variety,* about actress Jane Fonda's support of the Black Panthers at a rally in Embassy Auditorium sponsored by the Committee United For Political Prisoners. (See pages 128-129 for a copy of the letter.)

Army Archerd had not fallen for Held's sleazy anonymous letter on Jane Fonda the way Joyce Haber had fallen for the letter on Jean Seberg. Jane Fonda is a strong person, and the outcome of the FBI's attack upon her was not as drastic as in Seberg's case.

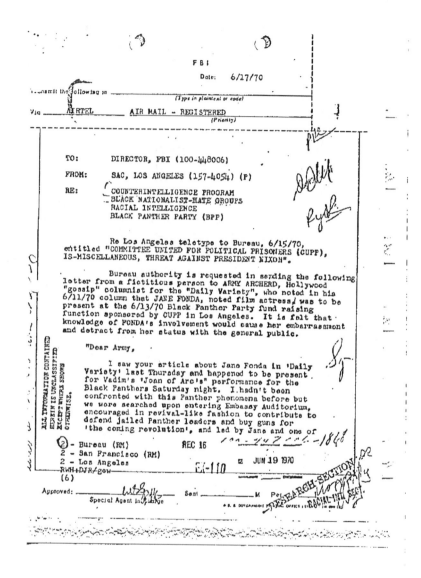

FBI

Date: 6/17/70

Transmit the following in
_____
(Type in plaintext or code)

Via ___ AIRTEL ___ AIR MAIL – REGISTERED
_____
(Priority)

TO: DIRECTOR, FBI (100-448006)

FROM: SAC, LOS ANGELES (157-4054) (P)

RE: COUNTERINTELLIGENCE PROGRAM
        BLACK NATIONALIST-HATE GROUPS
        RACIAL INTELLIGENCE
        BLACK PANTHER PARTY (BPP)

Re Los Angeles teletype to Bureau, 6/15/70,
entitled "COMMITTEE UNITED FOR POLITICAL PRISONERS (CUPP),
IS-MISCELLANEOUS, THREAT AGAINST PRESIDENT NIXON".

Bureau authority is requested in sending the following
letter from a fictitious person to ARMY ARCHERD, Hollywood
"gossip" columnist for the "Daily Variety", who noted in his
6/11/70 column that JANE FONDA, noted film actress, was to be
present at the 6/13/70 Black Panther Party fund raising
function sponsored by CUPP in Los Angeles. It is felt that
knowledge of FONDA's involvement would cause her embarrassment
and detract from her status with the general public.

"Dear Army,

I saw your article about Jane Fonda in 'Daily
Variety' last Thursday and happened to be present
for Vadim's 'Joan of Arc's" performance for the
Black Panthers Saturday night. I hadn't been
confronted with this Panther phenomena before but
we were searched upon entering Embassy Auditorium,
encouraged in revival-like fashion to contribute to
defend jailed Panther leaders and buy guns for
'the coming revolution', and led by Jane and one of

(2) - Bureau (RM)   REC 16
2 - San Francisco (RM)
2 - Los Angeles   JUN 19 1970
RWH+DJR/gow   EX-110
(6)

Approved: _____ Sent _____ M Per _____
          Special Agent in Charge

Richard Wallace Held's letter to Hoover, requesting permission to send an anonymous letter to a Hollywood gossip columnist about actress Jane Fonda's support of the Black Panthers.

LA 157-4054

the Panther chaps in a 'we will kill Richard
Nixon, and any other M_____ F_____ who stands in
our way' refrain (which was shocking to say the
least!). I think Jane has gotten in over her head
as the whole atmosphere had the 1930's Munich
beer-hall aura.

"I also think my curiosity about the Panthers has
been satisfied.

"Regards,

/s/ "Morris"

    Usual precautions would be taken by the Los
Angeles Division to preclude identification of the Bureau
as the source of the letter if approval is granted.

- 2*-

C h a p t e r   1 4

My 25-Year Award

A Tabloid of Obstructing Justice

After reading tens of thousands of classified documents on the FBI's COINTELPRO, from the 1950s to 1977, during my last months in the bureau, I was totally and completely disgusted with the FBI. I was ashamed to tell new friends and acquaintances in the Marina and at the California Yacht Club, where I spent most of my off hours, that I was an FBI agent. I went to the yacht club attempting to forget what I had read in the closed files that held the deadly secrets of COINTEL-PRO, many of which were released neither to the Church Committee nor to any court of law. I felt like a prisoner unable to escape the reality and horror of it all. It was agonizing to know just how evil the FBI was, when all the time it portrayed itself as the public's friend, the perfect image of law and order with justice for all.

I wanted to shout the truth to the world, but I doubted anyone would believe what I had to say about Hoover's untarnished FBI and his proclaimed immaculate conception.

The final disillusionment with the organization I once had loved and respected took place on April 11, 1977, the day I received my twenty-five-year key. Token emblems in twenty-four-carat gold were presented to agents at intervals of ten, twenty, twenty-five, thirty, thirty-five, and forty years of service. They were small enough to be attached to a key chain or mounted on the face of a ring, much like a college class ring. The keys varied in style and design, but they portrayed a scale of justice and the FBI motto of fidelity, bravery, and integrity. I had received my ten-year and twenty-year keys in an envelope in my mail folder. I expected little more for my twenty-five years of dedicated service. Much to my surprise I was invited to meet Special Agent in Charge of the Security Division Elmer Linberg in his private office. I had not been invited to Linberg's office before, so I did not know what to expect.

Linberg was nearing retirement, as was I, and so we had a lot in common. We reminisced about the good old days under J. Edgar Hoover when bag jobs and COINTELPRO were normal operations and no one dared to make scurrilous remarks about Hoover or the FBI.

Linberg sat behind his spotlessly clean mahogany executive desk, which went well with the walnut-paneled office. I sat on the brown leather couch, which Elmer used for taking naps after lunch. We both sipped coffee served by Linberg's secretary. We were waiting for the photographer to arrive to take our pictures—of Linberg shaking my hand as he handed me my twenty-five-year key.

The American flag stood in the corner. A large FBI plaque hung on the wall behind Linberg, along with photographs of FBI Director Clarence Kelley, Attorney General Griffin Bell, and President Jimmy Carter. An autographed picture of J. Edgar Hoover sat on Linberg's desk. The room was filled with symbolic artifacts, almost to the point of nausea.

Linberg had the haggard look of a long-time bureaucrat as he reclined in his high-back leather chair. Deep wrinkles lined his face as though each year of bureau service had been etched with a scalpel. His voice cracked. He punctuated each remark with deliberate movements of his arms and hands as though directing an orchestra. It was easy to imagine that he had once been forceful in his younger years, but now the motions had the hollowness of a man just hanging on to the job until his mandatory retirement date of January 1, 1978.

Linberg sipped his coffee and said, "It was different when we joined the FBI, Wes. You remember how everyone thought so highly of Mr. Hoover and the FBI in the fifties? We had a fine public image then, didn't we Wes?"

"Yes, sir. We did." I smiled and nodded agreeably.

"What I can't understand is why the newspapers keep publishing all these derogatory stories about us. They must think they can't sell papers without taking pot shots at the FBI."

Linberg was incensed over the daily beating the FBI had been taking in the news for the more than two years since the Church Committee had exposed some of the FBI wrongdoing, abuse of power, and cover-up. Hardly a day passed without another revelation about FBI corruption. He leaned forward and slammed the desk with his fist. "Don't they realize that without the FBI this country would be overrun with communists? It's getting so we have to justify all of our investigations on these subversive bastards."

He leaned back, frustrated by the implications of his last statement. "We have to defend our image now because people are critical of everything the FBI does, everything we stand for."

Pausing for a moment, he looked at the National Cemetery across the street with row after row of grave markers for the fighting men who had given their lives for their country. He turned back to me and said, "What really gets me, Wes, is that it's not fair to the thousands of agents like yourself who have given years of faithful, dedicated service to mold this great organization."

"You're absolutely right, sir." Linberg had every reason to believe I was sympathetic to his defense of the FBI. I was, after all, a twenty-five-year veteran with a good conduct record. I had been a loyal organization man who followed orders—even when it meant breaking the law—right up to the end. It was difficult for me to conceal my disgust at having to sit through Linberg's eulogy of Hoover and the FBI. It was annoying to sit there and listen to Linberg speak as though the FBI had done nothing wrong.

He said, "We must never forget the devoted leadership Mr. Hoover gave us all. He offered a firm hand when it was needed. Mr. Hoover set a splendid example for us all to follow. I hope we can instill the spirit of J. Edgar Hoover in all the new agents."

I wanted to stand up and shout him down. I wanted to pound his desk and shout that the FBI had violated every due process of law imaginable. I was mad as hell when no one had had the guts to call Clarence Kelley a liar when he had admitted publicly that the FBI had conducted only 238 surreptitious entries on fourteen targets between 1941 and 1966. But I had decided a few weeks earlier that my twenty-fifth anniversary would be my last. I was determined not to get into an argument with Linberg. I wanted to retire on May 20, 1977, the day I turned fifty and would become eligible to retire.

Linberg was impatient. He punched the intercom. "Where is that photographer? He was supposed to be here ten minutes ago!"

His secretary answered, "He just called to say he'd be right down, sir."

Linberg continued his diatribe on FBI critics. "You know what really bothers me? Its the Freedom of Information Act. It is going to destroy the bureau if we have to turn over all those files in the Chief Clerk's office. People already know about the Weatherman bag jobs. What if they find out about the thousands we did in the forties and fifties?"

I wanted to laugh and clap. I felt like dancing a jig, but I remained deadpan. "Yeah, we had a bag job squad of twenty-four agents in Chicago in the fifties. I certainly wouldn't want that to come out."

"Well," said Linberg, with a show of one-upmanship, "we had thirty-five agents on our bag job squad here in LA back then."

I could not argue against bag jobs with Linberg because he had stated during an all-agents conference in September 1975, just two months after the first public disclosure of FBI break-ins, that the FBI should get back into bag jobs in the counterintelligence field. I had been able to rationalize bag jobs in the 1950s when I was young and naive, but I now believed we should not have done them at all, and I was determined not to defend them in 1977.

In the midst of our mostly one-sided conversation, the telephone rang. Linberg answered, then paused. "Hello, Andy. How's everything at the bureau?" Linberg covered the phone and whispered, "It's Andy Decker."

Linberg and Decker continued talking. Andy Decker was the Assistant Director in Charge of the Computer Systems Division in Washington, D.C.

"No problem at all, Andy. I was thinking that we'd better make the agents out here aware of the situation."

Linberg frowned. "That's right. The statute of limitations hasn't expired for a few of them. Those are the ones we have to worry about." He jotted some notes on a yellow-lined pad. "You're 100% right, Andy. The agents have to get together on their stories or we'll all go down the tube. I'll touch base with the ones out here. Don't worry. We won't have anybody admitting that we did any bag jobs out here in the seventies."

Linberg completed his call and hung up the phone. He said, "That was Andy Decker. We were talking about the Weatherman bag jobs."

"Yes, sir. I thought so."

"This Justice Department investigation that's going on could become quite a problem if some agent decides to blow the whistle. I'm sure you understand it's a delicate situation."

"Yes, very delicate." I quickly calculated the number of years since I last had done a Weatherman bag job. The statute of limitations had expired.

Linberg asked if I had been involved in any bag jobs in New York. I had been in 1970. They were Weatherman related, just after the Townhouse explosion, but I lied to Linberg. I told him I had worked stolen cars and bombing matters in New York. I did not admit to any bag jobs in New York or Los Angeles because, frankly, I did not trust Linberg or Andy Decker any farther than I could spit into a hurricane.

Linberg said, "It's unfortunate for some of those fellows. We'll do the best we can to protect them."

That is when I felt like taking out my .38 Colt and shooting the bastard's nuts off. Linberg must have thought he was talking to a first office agent just out of training school. He was not trying to protect any agent; he was protecting himself and his pension. The special agents in charge of the offices and the assistant directors in charge of divisions at the bureau were the ones who had ordered the brick agents to do the Weatherman bag jobs. Linberg was trying to make it sound as if the brick agents had thought up the idea of black bag jobs. I didn't know how much more of his bullshit rhetoric I could handle before exposing my feelings and jeopardizing my own pension, which was just a month away. I remembered my feelings in training school when I first had seen FBI wrongdoing and what I had done to survive. I knew I could hold on until the photographer arrived.

Linberg continued as though he was talking to Hoover, whose picture sat on the desk in front of him, instead of talking to me. "Things were simpler when we entered the FBI. We didn't have to worry about interference from the attorney general. We could carry out our mission without all this damned political interference."

That was exactly why the FBI was having problems with Congress and the Department of Justice—because we did not worry about interference from the attorney general. Linberg had obviously divorced himself from the Department of Justice years ago and was now living in a state of adultery, forgetting that the FBI worked under the direction of the Department of Justice, not vice versa. I nodded in agreement like the good sycophant I had been for twenty-five years.

The photographer arrived and took our pictures in front of the FBI plaque and the American flag with Linberg handing me the twenty-five-year key in an envelope.

When I returned to my desk, I sat and looked at the gold token which represented my twenty-five years of dedicated service. I was mad as hell at what the FBI had done to my integrity. I felt betrayed by the FBI. I had just heard two top FBI officials talking about covering up Weatherman bag jobs in an effort to protect themselves from prosecution and I had not had the guts to voice an objection. For months I had hoped someone with the guts of William W. Turner would step forward and blow the whistle. I had dismissed the thought of doing it myself because I knew what had happened to whistle-blowers in the government. I could not financially afford to do what Turner had done in 1961. Also, I had been afraid to alienate my FBI friends who would write me off if I broke the unspoken secret code of silence. I had not wanted to embarrass my family by denouncing what they had considered a proud and successful career in the FBI.

I called a friend in the New York FBI office, Terry Roberts, with whom I had worked on the Sam Melville bombings and who was instrumental in the successful surveillance the night Melville was arrested. I had worked with Terry Roberts for a short time on the Weathermen after the Townhouse explosion, before leaving on transfer to Los Angeles. I admired and respected Terry Roberts as a friend and as an FBI agent.

When Terry answered the telephone I told him I had just received my twenty-five-year key and that I was planning to retire next month.

Terry answered, "Congratulations, you lucky bastard."

There was momentary silence, as if we had been cut off. Then Terry continued, "I have just been indicted, along with dozens of other agents, for illegal wiretaps and bag jobs on the Weathermen."

I had read in the newspaper about possible indictments against FBI agents in New York who had conducted Weatherman bag jobs and illegal wiretaps. I was concerned, but I was relieved when my name was not among those listed. I knew many of those named in the paper. When I had read the news reports, I had thought the top officials at the bureau were the ones who should be indicted—not the agents.

Black bag jobs were the creation of top officials such as J. Edgar Hoover; Clyde Tolson; Alan H. Belmont, the head of the Domestic Intelligence Division in the 1950s; W.R. Glavin, head of the Administrative Division in the 1950s; John P. Mohr, head of the Administrative Division in the 1960s; and William C. Sullivan, head of the Domestic Intelligence Division in the 1960s.

Terry said, "Wes, you don't know what the hell it feels like to see your name on an indictment."

I tried to imagine what it must be like. I had committed enough bag jobs for Hoover that if I were sentenced on local charges for each one, consecutively, I would have had to serve somewhere between 5,000 and 10,000 years behind bars. That was not a happy thought, when my purpose in joining the FBI had been to uphold the law.

I began to tell Terry about the conversation between Linberg and Decker, and about the agents named in the newspaper who had been indicted for bag jobs, but he cut me off.

"Wait a minute, Wes. I was one of those indicted. I think it would be improper for me to discuss the matter with anyone."

I continued to talk, but Terry cut me off again.

"You'd better be quiet, Wes."

"What?"

"Just don't discuss it with me. And you'd better not discuss it with your SAC because what Linberg and Decker were doing is obstruction of justice."

I started to laugh. "Don't be ridiculous." Then it hit me. Terry was a lawyer and he was right. The conversation I had witnessed constituted a conspiracy between two top FBI officials to have FBI agents alter their testimony before a federal grand jury—a crime punishable by a fine and imprisonment.

"I'm sorry for being so abrupt. I really can't talk anymore. I think my phone is bugged. The bureau is trying to stop any conspiracy among agents to tell the truth before the grand jury. They want to be alerted in advance so they can take whatever action is necessary."

I don't recall hanging up the telephone. I sat stunned. I could not believe I had been so corrupted over the years that I had been blind to the illegal cover-up and obstruction of justice. It was more like the little white lies that the FBI tells on a regular basis to protect and enhance its image. Lying was such a daily routine, from the time we signed in in the morning until the time we went home at night, that Linberg and Decker's obstruction of justice went right over my head as just another untruth.

I realized that after twenty-five years I could not tell the difference between absolute right and absolute wrong. Somehow I did sense what was wrong, but in order to survive we had to stretch the truth, and in so doing it became easy to color the truth so that it appeared as though we were not lying. This approach was necessary within the FBI in order to maintain our image of perfection.

After talking with Terry Roberts, I knew that the top officials, who had authorized the illegal wiretaps and bag jobs, were going to hang out to dry the brick agents who did the illegal wiretaps and bag jobs. I knew the top officials would lie to protect themselves just as they had done for a quarter century. I knew that when it came time to fish or cut bait, my friends in New York such as Terry Roberts would be put up for bait. I knew that the agents would be called rogue agents out of control. This is what we were told in Chicago in the 1950s would happen if we were ever caught doing a bag job. Hoover would have disowned us and we would be selling pencils on a street corner.

After talking with Terry Roberts, I knew that I had to tell the truth about the FBI's wrongdoing in an attempt to protect the many dedicated agents who would follow in our footsteps. Unless something changed, new agents would do what we had done thinking it was the correct thing to do to preserve our democracy. Top officials would approve of the actions, rationalizing that it is consistent with their mandate to stay on top of subversion and political unrest.

I began immediately to make notes of FBI wrongdoing, starting with the conversation I had heard between Linberg and Andy Decker. I made notes of what Terry Roberts had said. Then I began to make notes on what I remembered about wrongdoing over my entire career. I used the office dictaphones as I reviewed COINTEL-PRO files for about one month.* I did not yet know what to do with the information I had collected.

I discussed the matter privately with my brother Tom. He agreed to have one of his secretaries type up the information I had dictated to tape cassettes.

I was aware of the legal problems involved with whistle-blowing when the *New York Times* published "The Pentagon Papers." Daniel Ellsberg had released to the press information about the Pentagon and the Vietnam war. He did not take actual documents, just the information. I followed Ellsberg's cue and took only information from FBI files which documented FBI wrongdoing.

After my retirement I set out to find a good attorney who could represent me in exposing the FBI's corruption and cover-up without ending up in trouble myself. I had good reason for concern about my safety. The FBI is ruthless in dealing with anyone who attempts to expose its own wrongdoing. William W. Turner is a good example of an agent who was fired for blowing the whistle.

---

* I continued to review FBI FOIA documents for about five years after I retired.

Chapter 15

Streetfighter in the Courtroom

I retired on my fiftieth birthday on Friday, May 20, 1977. I busied myself for the next few weeks putting together a 212-page manuscript of notes I had typed in the dinette of our sailboat and my brother's office had typed in Riverside. I called it "FBI Chicanery."

In June I spoke with Tom Kerr, who was retired and was living in an apartment at the Bar Harbor marina complex where Paula and I kept our sailboat. We were in the hot-tub having cocktails one evening when Kerr and I discussed the ongoing Department of Justice investigation of FBI break-ins against the Weathermen. Kerr said that Wendell Stone was back in Washington, D.C., testifying before a federal grand jury about his knowledge of Weatherman bag jobs in Los Angeles. Kerr said he did not think Stone would open his mouth about any of the bag jobs.

Kerr said that when the departmental attorney in charge of the Special Litigation Unit, Guy Goodwin, had been in Los Angeles in 1970 to prepare for the "Tucson Five" grand jury, Goodwin had told him that he did not care how Kerr got the information on the Weathermen. Kerr quoted Goodwin as saying, "Just get it."

It was rumored that Kerr's "beards" had done several bag jobs, but I wanted to get Kerr's response, so I said, "But the squad never pulled any bag jobs or did anything illegal, did it?"

Kerr laughed and said, "That's what I like to hear, we never did anything wrong." Kerr shook his head. "Wes, you don't know the half of it. The 'beards' were out there pulling bag jobs all the time; it was just that no one in the office knew about it. It was like the fifties all over again."

Kerr was upset because the Department of Justice was trying to railroad some of the agents after Goodwin had given them approval to do the bag jobs on the Weathermen. Kerr said, "I have volumes of notes that will blow Guy Goodwin and his whole damned Department of Justice right out of the water if they ever prosecute the first FBI agent for doing bag jobs. If they so much as touch an agent, I will put the whole goddamned department behind bars."

I asked Kerr about the bag job we had done on Donald Mohs in Santa Barbara. Kerr said, "No one is mentioning the Donald Mohs caper in 1971."

Kerr added that the grand jury in Washington, D.C. was not calling retired agents to testify. I had hoped that I would be called to testify because then I could have testified to the truth about the break-ins. But I was never given the chance to tell the grand jury what I knew.

I spoke to an agent who had done bag jobs on the Weathermen with me in 1970, Wendell Stone, on July 1, 1977, after he had returned from Washington. He said he had testified before the grand jury and that he was asked whether he knew of any break-ins by the FBI against the Weathermen in Los Angeles. Stone said he told the grand jury that he did not know of any. Stone laughed and said, "The grand jury doesn't know the right questions to ask." He laughed again and said, "I didn't tell them about Willie-the-Pick."

Another agent on the squad was nick-named "Willie-the-Pick" because of the many break-ins he allegedly had supervised. I was not privy to "Willie-the-Pick's" break-ins, so I cannot comment on his successes. However, if he had obtained any information as to the whereabouts of any of the Weatherman fugitives, I would have known immediately because the major fugitive cases had been assigned to me.

Wendell Stone had not told the grand jury about the break-ins we had done together on the residence of suspected Weathermen Robert Gottlieb and Susan Sutheim, or the ones we had done jointly on Elizabeth Stanley, another suspected Weatherman, with other agents.

Stone confirmed what Kerr had said about the grand jury not calling retired agents. He said, "If they do call you, just don't admit to anything, because they can't prove it."

On September 27, 1977, I submitted to the FBI a Freedom of Information Act request for my personnel files.

That fall I attended a seminar on the subject of government conspiracy at the University of Southern California, Los Angeles, under the direction of Professor Donald Freed. Now that I was a private citizen, I wanted to hear Freed's thoughts on CIA and FBI conspiracies.

After the series of lectures ended, I approached Freed and told him that I was a retired FBI agent. I was apprehensive about his reaction to me since it was the FBI who had attempted to have him assassinated by creating the flyer calling him a police pig and had had him fired from several jobs.

Donald Freed was a gentleman, always smiling when we talked. Although he did not say so, I had the impression that he thought FBI agents are lacking mentally.

When I told him I was writing a manuscript on FBI wrongdoing, he offered suggestions for my writings. We met several times, and he told me later that he had written a novel based on my life experiences. *The Spymaster* was published in 1980.

In October, Paula and I chartered a thirty-four-foot bare boat sailboat for three weeks in the British Virgin Islands, which means we sailed and did our own cooking. On our way back from the Virgin Islands we stopped in New York City for a few days. I attempted to contact the renowned attorney Leonard Boudin, even though the FBI thought him to be a communist, but he was not available.

Donald Freed suggested that I contact the renowned Charles R. Garry of San Francisco, who had just written his own book, titled *Streetfighter in the Courtroom.*

I met Garry in November 1977. It was a traumatic experience because I had known about Garry from my FBI days in Chicago when he made numerous legal assaults on the loyalty oath during the McCarthy era. Even then I had agreed with what Garry had to say to the House Un-American Activities Committee. Garry had been vehemently opposed to legislation like the Broyles Bill in Illinois.

Garry had represented clients whom Hoover considered dangerous and subversive. He had defended FBI COINTELPRO targets and Security Index subjects such as Huey Newton for the murder of an Oakland cop, and Bobby Seale for murder and kidnapping in New Haven, Connecticut.

Mr. Garry had wanted to represent Bobby Seale in 1969 on charges of conspiracy growing out of the 1968 Democratic Convention riots, but he had developed a painful gall bladder condition that required surgery. Chicago's Federal Judge Julius Hoffman had denied Garry a six-week postponement, even though Hoffman had granted another attorney, in another case, a three-month delay so that the attorney and his wife could take a trip to the South Seas.

Garry told me that six weeks to the day after the Chicago case began, he was back to work in the San Francisco court representing other clients. Bobby Seale was later severed from the Chicago case and was sentenced to four years in prison for contempt for disturbing Judge Hoffman during the proceedings. As Charles said, "Bobby Seale was jailed for demanding his constitutional right to an attorney of his own choosing."

Meeting the great Charles Garry for the first time was startling for me, not because of his fame and success in the courtroom, but because I had always been on the "right side of the law" and he was on the other side. The FBI had pegged Garry as a dangerous member of the Communist Party and tabbed him DETCOM on the Security Index, to be arrested in the event of a national emergency.

I wanted to take the matter of FBI chicanery to the Attorney General of the United States. I felt that Garry, who later became my dearest friend and confidant, could best represent me to the Department of Justice.

The House Select Committee on Intelligence had provided the Department of Justice with information in 1975 that FBI officials were allegedly profiting from the bureau's business transactions with its exclusive electronics equipment supplier. Attorney General Edward H. Levi had requested that FBI Director Clarence Kelley investigate these allegations. The FBI had investigated itself and submitted a report which Levi found to be incomplete and unsatisfactory. That should not have been a surprise to anyone. Anytime the FBI investigates itself, it will lie to no end to protect its contrived image.

Displeased with the report, Edward Levi had directed the Office of Professional Responsibility and the Criminal Division of the Department of Justice to conduct their own independent investigation.

In January 1978, the Department of Justice released a forty-page report which I hoped would disclose the FBI's wrongdoing and enable something to be done about it.

Their report revealed that top FBI officials had wrongfully accepted gratuities, improperly diverted government funds for FBI public relations, and illegally received goods and services. The Department of Justice took no action against the officials. More specifically, the report showed that:

1. John P. Mohr, Assistant Director in Charge of the Administrative Division and the Assistant to the Director, had violated the law by accepting gratuities, using Confidential Fund monies for unauthorized purposes, and accepting paid hunting trips at Remington Farms, owned by an FBI arms supplier. He was not prosecuted.

2. Nicholas P. Callahan, former Assistant Director of the Administrative Division and later Associate Director, had improperly diverted thousands of dollars of the employees' Recreation Fund, known as the FBIRA, and Confidential Fund monies for unauthorized FBI public relations activities. Callahan admitted receiving FBI goods and services. FBI employees had decorated his beach house and built a fence, walnut shelves, and other furniture for his residence.

3. Ivan W. Conrad, Assistant Director of the FBI Laboratory, had taken pieces of electronic equipment for use in his own home.

4. Clarence M. Kelley, FBI Director, had received goods and services from the FBI. He was permitted to reimburse the bureau for the services and goods he received.

5. G. Speights McMichael had been in charge of the FBI's Property Procurement and Management Section and had been in charge of the Imprest Fund. He had accepted a paid hunting trip to Remington Farms. McMichael had neglected his responsibilities in managing the Imprest Fund and had permitted violations of procurement procedures.

The Department of Justice investigation also revealed that between September 1951 and June 1972, Nicholas P. Callahan had obtained $39,590 from the FBIRA designated for the "Library Fund."

(The FBI Recreation Association was founded in 1931 for the purpose of promoting and encouraging athletic, social, and welfare activities among its members.) The association's records contain no explanation or authorization for these disbursements. Mr. Callahan was the Library Fund's only recipient and maintained the only records of its expenditures. Shortly after Hoover died, Mr. Callahan and Mr. Mohr discontinued the fund and destroyed its records. Neither of the two FBIRA treasurers who served during this period knew why the fund was named the "Library Fund" in the FBIRA Disbursements Journal.

Only Hoover, Tolson, Callahan, Mohr, and the treasurers knew about the Library Fund. Disbursements were made to the fund without the authorization of FBIRA officers, whose approval is required under the FBIRA charter. Nicholas Callahan asserted that the disbursements were for official public relations for which appropriated funds are unavailable under law.

The investigation also revealed that $55,849 of FBIRA funds had been expended illegally on receptions for the National Academy. The receptions were not FBIRA activities and they were not open to FBIRA members. Griffin B. Bell, then attorney general, said the Department of Justice investigation was "intended to assure the nation that the Department of Justice can investigate and police itself." Bell was correct that the Department of Justice could investigate itself. However, it wasn't so clear that it would take action against its own kind when it found chicanery and wrongdoing. Neither Callahan nor Mohr were prosecuted for their illegal expenditures from the FBIRA's funds, although Callahan was asked to resign. Conrad, Kelley, and McMichael were also not prosecuted.

Up until the time I had read the Department of Justice report, I debated whether I should expose FBI corruption. Now I knew what I needed to do.

During the past year I had had countless nightmares and I often awoke in a cold sweat. My distorted and disjointed dreams took me back to my childhood in elementary school. I questioned my friends about what I should do. Some said I should tell the truth. Others said I should forget everything I knew about corruption because no one really cares. Still others said I would lose every friend I ever had.

The sleepless nights and nightmares continued as I asked my friends in high school, in college, and in the FBI about what I should do. Their answers were always the same. What became important to me was what I thought of myself as a human being. I realized that if I were ever to have any self-respect I had to square my experience in the FBI with my conscience and my country.

I recalled what my father used to say when I was a boy. Dad was a public school administrator and a teacher of mathematics, chemistry, and physics. He said the laws of nature are always true. Dad was a deacon in the church. He taught Sunday School and occasionally gave sermons for the preacher or minister if they were ill or out of town. Dad used to tell me that the truth shall make me free, as he paraphrased from the Bible, *John* 8:32. He frequently told me as a little boy that truth is great and mighty above all things. Again he quoted the Bible, *I Esdras* 4:41. Dad also quoted an ancient Latin Proverb that I shall never forget, "Truth brings forth hatred."

I did many things with my father as a boy. We hunted rabbit, squirrel, quail, and pheasant on my uncle's farm in Ohio. We fished, we worked our backyard vegetable garden, and we played. I was his caddie and ball finder when he played golf with members of the school board in Salineville, Ohio, where he was superintendent of schools for several years. My reward as caddie after eighteen holes was a bottle of orange soda.

Dad died in 1974, so I couldn't ask him what I should do. But I knew what he would say if I had.

I was furious with the Department of Justice report because the top FBI officials had gotten off scot-free. Callahan and Mohr had gotten stolen money in the FBIRA fund from clerical employees, other agents, and from me for twenty-one years, and they had not gotten so much as a slap on the wrist, while all the time Callahan and Mohr had been disciplining agents for being a few pounds overweight, for being below the office average overtime, or for some other nit-picky reason.

If any agent had taken money from the FBIRA fund, he would have been fired and prosecuted. Agent *Bill Libby* was the newly elected president of the FBIRA fund in Chicago in 1958. When Libby had asked the bureau for an audit of the FBIRA funds, which no agent had ever done, John Mohr transferred Libby from Chicago. That was the end of any requests for an audit, which would have exposed Callahan and Mohr as embezzlers.

I went to the telephone and called Charles Garry.

"Charles, this is Wes Swearingen."

"Yes, Wes. How are you?"

"Fine Charles. I'm calling about Attorney General Bell's statement in the paper that the Justice Department can police itself. Did you see it?"

"Yes, I did."

"Since there was no prosecution on any of the violations, I would like to send the attorney general some matters they can prosecute, if they have a mind to. What do you think?"

"I think that's a good idea. Send me what you want him to have and I'll send it on to him under my letterhead, that way we will get a response. If you send it to the department they may just bury it." (See page 149 for Garry's letter.)

Garry did not sound hopeful that the Department of Justice would do anything. I sent him two lists of twenty-five allegations of corruption. One list had twelve allegations of minor fraud and corruption. The other had thirteen allegations of top FBI officials who had perjured themselves before the U.S. Congress and in federal court.

When Garry sent me a copy of his letter to Bell, I knew there was no turning back. I thought of the "Truth brings forth hatred" quote my father had used. It was not long before this proverb became a reality.

A month had passed since Garry had written to Bell, and still there was no answer. I thought that Bell had ignored Garry's letter just as he said Bell might. I called Garry again to remind him that it had been a month since he had written to Bell. I asked, "What can we do now?"

Garry said, "I've discussed your situation with Dave Dellinger. You've heard of him." He laughed, knowing very well that every FBI agent had heard of the radical leftist who had been indicted in Chicago on charges of conspiracy growing out of the 1968 Democratic Convention riots.

LAW OFFICES OF

GARRY, DREYFUS, McTERNAN, BROTSKY, HERNDON & PESONEN, INC.

1256 MARKET STREET AT CIVIC CENTER

SAN FRANCISCO 94102

(415) 864-3131

CABLE ADDRESS: "DAYCAP"

CHARLES R. GARRY
BENJAMIN DREYFUS
FRANCIS J. McTERNAN
ALLAN BROTSKY
JAMES HERNDON
DAVID E. PESONEN
BRIAN E. WALSH

OF COUNSEL
DONALD L. A. REASON
COLLEEN G. HAAS

SAN JOSE OFFICE
255 SO. MARKET STREET
SAN JOSE 95113
(408) 286-9222

January 30, 1978

PERSONAL AND CONFIDENTIAL:

Honorable Griffin B. Bell
Attorney General of the United States
U. S. Department of Justice
Washington, D.C. 20535

Dear Sir:

This office represents a former FBI agent with
many years of service, who believes that for years the
Bureau has violated every form of due process of law in
its endeavors. If proper assurances of sincere investigation are forthcoming, he is willing, through his attorney,
to cooperate, but not until then.

The attached exhibit "A" from my client should
enable you to see that my client knows what he is talking
about.

As you can see, the corruption is continuing even
under the directorship of Clarence Kelley. As my client
points out, Mr. Kelley and his subordinates have given
false testimony before the U.S. Senate. He points out
that the matters he has listed are relatively minor compared
to the information not yet revealed and still within the
statute of limitations.

I will be available to meet with you and you alone,
on this matter.

Very truly yours,

CHARLES R. GARRY

CRG:bw
Enclosure

Attorney Charles Garry's letter to Judge Griffin B. Bell.

In 1968, the FBI had tabbed Dave Dellinger as a "Key Activist" on the Security Index. He had also been a target of the FBI's Top Secret COINTELPRO, with orders from Director Hoover that Dellinger, a New Left organizer, be neutralized. Judge Hoffman, the judge who first had heard the case of the Chicago Seven, had assisted Hoover and the FBI by giving Dellinger six months in jail for calling him "Mister" Hoffman. Hoffman subsequently had given five of the Chicago Seven sentences of five years in prison and $5,000 fines. The Ninth Circuit Court of Appeals realized that Hoffman had used the court system to carry out one of Hoover's many sadistic vendettas, and so it overturned all of Judge Hoffman's contempt charges and convictions.

I wondered what kind of a stunt Garry was trying to pull by having me talk to Dave Dellinger. I wanted to talk to the Attorney General of the United States, not to some radical from the sixties. I answered, "Yes, I have heard of Dave Dellinger."

Garry said, "He would like to talk to you."

"I don't know. That's not what I had in mind." Actually, I was afraid to talk to Dellinger, but I knew that the story of FBI corruption would never get out if I left it up to the Department of Justice. The FBI had given Dave Dellinger a hard time under COINTELPRO, and I thought Dave might be out for revenge and use me as a whipping boy.

Garry said, "You don't have to decide anything right now. Just meet with him and we'll talk. If you don't like him or don't trust him, we'll drop it right there. He won't print anything you or I disagree with."

"That sounds fair enough."

"O.K., buddy. I'll set up an appointment. The three of us will meet in my office. We will agree on the ground rules before you two begin to discuss anything about the FBI."

"That's O.K. Let me know what Dave says."

I met Dave Dellinger in Charles Garry's office. Garry set the ground rules and then Dellinger and I went to a secure room and began our discussion of the FBI. The following is what Dellinger wrote as an introduction to his story in the March 21, 1978, issue of *Seven Days* magazine:

Early in March I received a long distance call from a lawyer who said, "I have a client, a former FBI agent, who is very upset by the illegal activities of the FBI and their continued cover-up. He has had some disillusioning experiences and wants to tell the American public about them but he's concerned about his safety. Although he has no proof, he doesn't believe that William Sullivan [former number three man in the bureau] died in a hunting accident. From his 25 years experience in the FBI, he's convinced that Sullivan was murdered to prevent him from testifying before Congress, and he doesn't want to become a target for accidents himself."

The caller went on to say that the agent knew me from his FBI work and would like to meet with me. "I don't know how much he will be willing to say for publication, but I think it would be worthwhile for the three of us to sit down together to see if there is a way that he can begin to get his story out without undue risk."

A few days later we met. For security reasons we met not in the city in which he lives nor in New York, where I live, but in a neutral setting. I was reminded of earlier meetings I had had with fugitives from the law—blacks in the South during civil rights days, deserters and draft resisters during the Vietnam war, and more recently with my colleague Abbie Hoffman of the Chicago Seven. This was my first surreptitious meeting with a disillusioned FBI agent but almost everything else was the same, including the need to take precautions against detection by the FBI.

In the present instance, the former agent clearly had more to lose than I did, but as near as I could tell, I was the more suspicious. I weighed his every word and gesture against the possibilities of entrapment. Was he a double agent on a fishing expedition for some obscure missing link that would help the FBI in any one of a number of nefarious schemes? After several hours of mutual exploration and discussion, we felt sure enough of one another for him to speak and for me to turn on the tape recorder.

What impressed me most about the two days we spent together was this former FBI agent's down-to-earth description of the daily routine dishonesty, corruption and inefficiency of the FBI. The more he talked, the more I realized that ironically the FBI is a prime victim of the very capitalist ethic it is dedicated to defending: in brief, it's everyone for himself in a relentless struggle for more power, privilege and affluence than one's associates, not to mention rival agencies. He told about attempts, mostly successful, to pad payrolls, expense accounts, statistics on caseloads and convictions; he recalled information supposedly supplied by informants who, in many cases, don't even exist; he described exploitation of the informer, the criminal, the public and the courts alike. The former agent said that false information was supplied by the FBI to government investigatory agencies as well as to Congress, the press and the public.

A month after Dellinger's article appeared in *Seven Days* magazine, the attorney general sent representatives from the Office of Professional Responsibility to speak to me in Garry's office. I outlined several minor allegations of fraud and produced some copies of documents to prove my allegations. Instead of being interested in FBI corruption, the OPR officials put me on the defensive by telling me that I was technically in violation of the law. I had taken copies of documents on FBI corruption and given them to the Department of Justice, and I was suddenly the one who was in trouble.

I recognized the old con game immediately. I had once reported the wrongdoing of a new agent who was under my supervision in London, Kentucky, to the Special Agent in Charge of the Louisville office. The Special Agent in Charge had told me to drop the matter, and I was threatened with administrative action for not having reported the matter to him by telephone instead of waiting to tell him in person in his office behind closed doors.

Four months after I had spoken to representatives of the Office of Professional Responsibility, they informed me that their investigation had been completed. They took no action against any of the top officials in my allegations. Again, I recognized the old cover-up. I decided not to go any further with the Office of Professional Responsibility or the Department of Justice.

Dellinger's *Seven Days* article attracted attention, and by June I had received a contract from the publisher William Morrow and Company, Inc. to do a book about my experiences in the FBI.

In September, just five months after having spoken with Dave Dellinger, the ancient Latin proverb that Dad had told me about slapped me in the face. *Jonathan Reid*, an FBI agent friend of mine in *Galisteo,* California, told me that *Fred Hamm*, of the Galisteo Police Department, had offered to "take care" of me if the FBI gave the word. This was my first death threat for exposing FBI corruption.

I was surprised that Jonathan Reid had told me about the possibility of a hit on me. Reid suggested that I talk to a major newspaper such as the *New York Times* in an effort to scare off any would-be assassins. I took my friend's warning and tried, from then on, to be in the company of others who could be witnesses to whatever might happen. I remembered what had happened to William C. Sullivan, and so I decided not to go on any hunting trips alone.

On December 13, 1978, a friend told me that the FBI was investigating me. He said that they had asked him if he had ever heard me using a typewriter on the boat. My friend had responded by asking the FBI agent, "Is it a crime to have a typewriter?"

I did not know what to expect, so that night I took all my notes and papers off the boat and out of a storage locker across the street and left them in a local attorney's office. I left the typewriter on board the boat along with a list of FBI informers who had testified in federal court and before the Congress of the United States. I had obtained the names from newspapers such as the *Los Angeles Times*. Also, I left a draft copy of Dellinger's article on the boat.

On December 14, 1978, all hell broke loose. Ten FBI agents swooped down, as if from trees, and raided our forty-three-foot sailboat, which Paula and I were preparing for a cruise to Hawaii. Two agents came on board wearing hard leather shoes. They asked me to sign a "Consent to Search" form to search the boat. They must have thought I was dense or had taken leave of my senses. I did not sign the consent form because a consent to search cannot be attacked in court. Then one of the agents whipped out a search warrant signed by Federal Magistrate John R. Kronenberg.

I immediately called Charles Garry in San Francisco because the FBI had said they also had a search warrant for Garry's office and that they were going to back a truck up to his office and take every damned file on his clients. When I told Garry what the FBI had said, he responded, "They are like hell!"

Then six more FBI agents came on board the boat in leather sole shoes and proceeded to tear apart every compartment and locker. I watched one FBI agent search Paula's locker and pull out her clothes to examine each pair of panties, each brassiere, each pair of socks and shoes as if they contained KGB secrets. The agent who fondled Paula's underclothes seemed to enjoy his work.

While all this was going on, two more obnoxious FBI agents took Paula to the Security Pacific National Bank on Admiralty Way to search our safe deposit box. The FBI goons itemized every document in the safe deposit box. One goon asked Paula if she would testify against me in a court of law.

Paula answered, "If you people had one-tenth of the integrity my husband has, he wouldn't be in the mess he's in right now. No, I won't testify against him!"

The majority of the documents described in the search warrant had been released to me under the Freedom of Information Act or had been turned over to the Church Committee during the hearings in 1975. Other documents described were the ones I had given to the Office of Professional Responsibility. It was obvious that the FBI was on a fishing expedition.

The FBI seized my Smith-Corona portable typewriter, the list of informers who had testified in open court, and Dave Dellinger's rough-draft article. It took six agents three hours to search our sailboat, an area in square footage the size of the average living room. They were put out when they could not find more to seize.

The documents the FBI agents were looking for were in another safe deposit box at the City National Bank in Century City several miles away, which included a copy of my 212-page manuscript "FBI Chicanery."

When the FBI first arrived to raid our boat, I did not know whether the Office of Professional Responsibility had finked on me or whether it was a result of my having talked with Dave Dellinger. But the search party told me that copies of whistle-blowing documents, including "FBI Chicanery," had been found in the rubble of Jonestown, Guyana, several days earlier, where 900 members of the People's Temple had committed suicide or were murdered under the direction of Jim Jones.

The FBI search party on the boat accused Charles Garry of taking the papers to Jonestown and they suggested that I get another attorney. I recognized the old COINTELPRO trick because that is what the FBI had tried to do with Huey Newton and Bobby Seale when Garry had defended them in court.

I learned later that the People's Temple had also been clients of Garry, who had been in Jonestown at the time of the suicides. I concluded that somehow the People's Temple had done a bag job on my files in Garry's office, copied them, and had taken them to Jonestown.

After the FBI ended their raid on our boat, I flew to San Francisco. Ten FBI agents were rifling files in Garry's law offices without a search warrant when I arrived. One agent was reading a copy of "FBI Chicanery."

I knew what the agents were capable of doing to Garry's office, so I gave them what they wanted to see. I knew that if they took anything else from Garry's office at night without a "nighttime" search warrant, there would be hell to pay in federal court later. The agents left Garry's office around midnight after they had looked at the papers I had given them.

The news of the FBI raid on our sailboat and Garry's office hit the news media like a thunderbolt. I received calls from news organizations around the world. Mike Wallace of CBS's "60 Minutes" had Paula and me flown to New York City for a special interview. I had not slept for three days since the FBI raid on the boat, and I was not animated enough for Wallace's show, which was to be aired that weekend.

John Crewdson, a reporter for the *New York Times,* interviewed me in San Francisco in December after Charles Garry set the ground rules. I let Crewdson look at a copy of "FBI Chicanery."

A very good friend in Los Angeles let Paula and me use the family's hideaway condominium on Maui, Hawaii, for a week, to recover from the FBI's raid on the boat and the sudden barrage of reporters asking all kinds of personal questions about my life and my work in the FBI.

One night around 2:30 A.M. Hawaii time, I was awakened by a telephone call from one Douglas Cassel, who identified himself as a Chicago attorney who was representing a group of professional people in Chicago who were suing the FBI, the Chicago Police Department "Red Squad," and the U.S. military intelligence groups.

I first thought the call was from some wiseacre FBI agent waking me in the middle of the night because I had talked to Dave Dellinger and John Crewdson. After a few minutes, I realized Doug Cassel was serious and I picked up a pencil to make notes on a steno pad. Cassel wanted me to write out an affidavit of my FBI experiences and he wanted me to detail such things as bag jobs in Chicago.

The group Cassel represented was named Business and Professional People for the Public Interest (BPI). There was a sense of desperation in Cassel's voice. He said the BPI had filed a suit against the FBI and the Chicago Police Department four years ago. Although Judge Alfred Kirkland had held FBI agents in contempt of court in the past, the FBI was holding its ground in the case. Cassel said he was calling me to ask if I would send him an affidavit immediately, as a last-ditch stand, before Judge Kirkland ruled in the FBI's favor. The next day I faxed an affidavit from the business offices of the Rock Resort Hotel in Kapalua to the law offices of Schiff, Hardin and Waite in Chicago, and I mailed a copy of the affidavit to Cassel.

After I returned from Hawaii, Cassel called me on our boat in Marina Del Rey. He profusely praised my affidavit and thanked me for saving the BPI case against the FBI and the Chicago Police Department "Red Squad."

When I heard how happy Doug Cassel was about my affidavit, I knew that my efforts to go public against the FBI's corruption and chicanery had not been in vain.

Cassel said that the Business and Professional Interests had originally made twenty-one demands on the FBI that included the termination of all forms of surveillance and harassment tactics against individuals involved in political and civil activities. The BPI had claimed that the illegal gathering of information by the FBI and the Chicago Police was in violation of these citizens' First Amendment rights and that the break-ins or bag jobs were a violation of their Fourth Amendment rights. The FBI had refused to budge on any of the items. Cassel said that after Judge Kirkland had reviewed my affidavit and Kirkland had had a discussion with the FBI's legal counsel as to the contents of my affidavit, the FBI had conceded to one of the BPI demands.

Meanwhile, I was looking for a writer to help me with the book I had to deliver to William Morrow in about a year. One writer in San Francisco wanted to do the book, but he wanted the copyright to my life history, without having to pay me a single penny. I refused.

The publisher recommended a writer in Hollywood. I gave the writer some of my material to review and I paid her $500 to write a dozen pages to see whether she could handle the project. She failed miserably. I had written a better essay in 1942 when I was a freshman in Steubenville High School and had won the American Legion Essay Contest for it.

I was running short of time on the book contract with William Morrow. I found yet another writer who claimed he had been published. We worked out an arrangement, I paid him $3,400, and I thought the book was in good hands.

Paula and I sailed off to Hawaii just a few days before the start of the July 4, 1979, Transpac Yacht Race from Los Angeles to Honolulu, a distance of 2,225 miles. We had not been out to sea before, but both of us together had had some fifty years of sailing and racing experience. We had a sister ship to the sailboat that had won "First in Class" in the 1969 Transpac Race. We were confident that we could handle the crossing to Hawaii as long as the sailboats in the Transpac Race were behind us in case we needed help. We made it safely to Honolulu before some of the racing yachts arrived. We did almost as well as some of the hot racers, and we were just two senior citizens cruising the Pacific.

Two months before sailing into the sunset on our way to Hawaii, which has the greatest sunsets I have ever seen, I had appeared on NBC's "Tomorrow" show with Tom Snyder in Los Angeles. Snyder and I had discussed briefly the corruption in the FBI. Among other charges of wrongdoing, I had accused James B. Adams, then Deputy Associate Director of the FBI, of lying to the Church Committee in 1975.

During the period of 1978 to 1982, I helped several prominent individuals to decipher the FBI documents they had received through the Freedom of Information Act. Bert Schneider, a movie producer, hired me to explain the meaning of the FBI's investigation of him for supporting African Americans in the Los Angeles community. Attorneys for Jane Fonda hired me to review her FBI file. Meanwhile, Garry was attempting to make sense out of his own FBI file. Of particular interest to Charles was the FBI's surveillance of him during the trial of Bobby Seale in New Haven, Connecticut.

Garry suspected that his office space and his hotel room had been bugged and that his telephones had been tapped during the trial, which is totally illegal and would have resulted in a mistrial had the judge known about the surreptitious FBI bugs and wiretaps.

The FBI furnished thousands of pages of documents from Charles Garry's file dating back to when he had been the attorney for the West Coast labor leader Harry Bridges. The file also had information on Garry's defense of Japanese American citizens who had been corralled like cattle into concentration camps in the United States during World War II, just because they were of Japanese descent.

After looking at the first batch of FOIA files from New Haven, I said to Charles, "This is FBI poppycock." I told him to ask the Department of Justice for specific documents, by name. I knew that if a person does not name a document, the FBI will deny that it exists. Of course, anyone not having been in the FBI will not know the name of a particular document, and so the FBI will deny they have it.

During one FOIA file review in Los Angeles, at the request of attorney William Kunstler, Kunstler had asked for all information from FBI surveillances. The agents under my supervision for the FOIA review interpreted surveillance as meaning to be physically followed around town. I explained to the agents the dictionary meaning of surveillance, which I am sure was what Kunstler had had in mind. Kunstler was furnished everything the Los Angeles office had on him.

After repeated FOIA requests and several reviews by me of Garry's file, the Department of Justice finally sent Charles Garry FBI documents revealing that Garry in fact had been illegally bugged and wiretapped during the whole period of the Bobby Seale trial in New Haven. The FBI had previously denied any wiretaps of Bobby Seale's defense camp.

After I had gone public in 1978 about FBI corruption, Stuart Hanlon, a San Francisco attorney, had contacted Garry to see if I would or could help Hanlon's client, Elmer "Geronimo" Pratt, who had been framed for murder by the FBI and the Los Angeles Police Department and who was still in jail. I knew from my experience on the Los Angeles Racial Squad and the review of COINTELPRO documents in 1977 that Elmer Pratt had been set up by the FBI because he was the charismatic leader of the Los Angeles Black Panther Party. The FBI had denied that Julius Carl Butler, who had testified against Pratt, was an FBI informer; that Pratt was the target of COINTELPRO; and that wiretaps existed which proved Pratt was innocent.

Stuart Hanlon had become Pratt's attorney sometime after Pratt had been convicted, and Hanlon was attempting to gain a release or a new trial for Pratt. The FBI stonewalled Hanlon and his assistant, Brian Glick, who later wrote a book titled *War at Home* (South End Press, Boston) just as they had stonewalled Johnnie L. Cochran, Jr. during Pratt's trial. (Cochran is now defending O.J. Simpson.) Hanlon and Glick had problems, understandably, with deciphering the FBI's heavily excised documents and with understanding the file codes and the FBI's secret code words for groups and classes of cases.

FBI Director William H. Webster announced in May 1980 that the FBI had conducted an "exhaustive" review of the Pratt case without interviewing any of the FBI agents involved who had tried to disrupt the Black Panther Party in the late 1960s and early 1970s.

I wrote a letter dated May 30, 1980, to Webster. I stated in part, "If it is true that the 'exhaustive' investigation did not include interviewing any of the FBI agents who tried to disrupt the Panthers in the late 1960s and early 1970s, then your credibility has fallen to new depths even beyond the imagination of Jules Verne." I ended my letter by writing, "Mr. Webster, you are either a fake or you are being deceived by your associates, if you think there has been an 'exhaustive' internal investigation into the Pratt case. Or could it be that you believe, as some others from squad two believe, that because a man is black he deserves to be in jail?"

Soon after my letter landed on Webster's desk, two FBI inspectors from Washington, D.C. landed at the Honolulu International Airport to interview me about Geronimo Pratt. I had planned to surreptitiously tape the interview so that I would have a recording of my statements because I knew how FBI agents twisted their reports to make themselves sound good and to report what the bureau wanted to hear. The hidden tape recorder was loaded and ready to go.

The first thing the Washington agents asked was whether I had a hidden tape recorder. The attorney, whose office we used, was a friend of Charles Garry. He put the kibosh on my recording of the interview by telling the FBI agents that I had a battery operated tape recorder in my briefcase. I felt like hitting Garry's friend alongside the head with a belaying pin.

I started the interview by saying that Pratt had been framed. The FBI agents denied it. I said Butler had been an informant and they denied that too. I told them that I had seen Butler's informant file when I was on the racial squad in Los Angeles. I also told them that the file had been closed during the trial and reopened after the trial. They nearly dropped their badges on the floor. One goon asked, "You saw Butler's informant file?"

I told the interviewing agents that Fred Hampton and Mark Clark had been set up for assassination by FBI agents in Chicago. They denied it and added that they were interested only in Geronimo Pratt.

When I told them that FBI informers George Stiner and Larry Stiner had assassinated Black Panther members Alprentice Carter and John Huggins on the UCLA campus on January 17, 1969, they responded by saying that no agent ever had arranged the assassination of anyone. I answered in anger, "How the hell would you know? You were not on the racial squad; fact is, you were not in the Los Angeles office. I was on the racial squad and I know what the hell I'm talking about."

The agents from Washington were interested only in hearing about Elmer Pratt. When the agents wrote their report about what I had said, it was so distorted that I did not recognize the interview report when I read it a few years later.

When I tried to give them information about the planned FBI assassinations, they responded by saying I should report it to the proper authorities. I said, "I thought the FBI was the proper authority."

After they terminated the interview, their parting question to me was, "How do you like retirement?"

I said, "I like it. It's better than what you two assheads are doing, covering up FBI wrongdoing."

While I basked on our yacht in a sun-drenched marina in Hawaii, the author I had paid to write my story was wallowing in the details of my life and my work in the FBI. After almost a year of mailing prose back and forth between Hawaii and California and $3,400 later, my so-called writer had no more to show for his effort than fifty pages. The editor at Morrow gave me ninety days to finish the project. I flew back to San Francisco, took my notes and papers from the writer, rented an apartment in Emeryville, rented an IBM Selectric typewriter, and proceeded to work day and night on the manuscript while Paula stayed on the yacht in Honolulu.

In less than sixty days I completed a 361-page manuscript of my experiences in the FBI. I submitted a copy of the manuscript to William Morrow publisher. I also sent a copy to FBI Director William Webster because, after William Turner had published his book *Hoover's FBI,* we in the FBI had had to send to the FBI anything we intended to have published so that they could review it for thirty days and censor anything that violated national security or was embarrassing to the FBI.

For reasons unknown to me, William Morrow turned down the manuscript after having paid me $7,500 to do the book. Morrow claimed the book was refused for business reasons. I suspect that the FBI got to someone at Morrow with the extortion tactics we in the FBI often used to squelch a book or a news story unfavorable to Hoover or the FBI. They had done this with William Turner's book, which Hoover had kept from publication for ten years, and had also driven the *Open City* newspaper out of business.

William Morrow had previously published books that were favorable to the FBI. Morrow had never published an exposé on Hoover or the FBI's wrongdoing. So I am not surprised that they reneged on their book contract. But as it turned out, my manuscript stirred up quite a hornet's nest, anyway.

Chapter 16

The Sweet Smell of Success

Charles Garry wanted me to testify in a court of law about FBI corruption, but I had no idea how I would get into court as a witness. I knew that if I did make it to a courtroom, no attorney could possibly ask the proper questions and I would not be able to volunteer information about corruption without an objection from some U.S. attorney. The FBI would certainly claim national security on nearly every issue.

When the FBI raided my boat, insulted my wife, searched our safe deposit box, and raided my attorney's office at night without a valid warrant, the idiotic FBI goons expected to walk away from all that as though nothing had ever happened. Well, something did happen. The FBI's stupidity on that day gave me a chance to go public and expose the FBI's corruption and wrongdoing in a manner that might not have been possible without the FBI's help.

Reporters from across the United States and from around the world wanted details about FBI corruption. Reporters from the *New York Times,* the *Los Angeles Times,* the *Los Angeles Herald Examiner,* the *San Francisco Chronicle,* the *Chicago Sun-Times,* the *Freedom News* (a publication of the Church of Scientology), and the Associated Press International, to mention just a few, interviewed me and wrote articles on FBI corruption and the COINTELPRO.

Perhaps the most ironic developments that resulted from the FBI's stupid raids on my boat and Garry's office are the ones surrounding the lawsuits brought against the FBI and the Department of Justice by the Business and Professional People for the Public Interest in Chicago, the family members of Fred Hampton and Mark Clark in Chicago, and the Socialist Workers Party (SWP) in New York City. In each case, the publicity that the raid gave me and my revelations of FBI misconduct led to information that I had provided being used in court against the bureau.

The Socialist Workers Party had filed a $40 million lawsuit against the FBI alleging that the FBI had used illegal tactics in the investigation of the party. The FBI stonewalled the SWP at every turn and even blew smoke screens in the face of Federal Judge Thomas P. Griesa, who was hearing the case. Stan Hunlast, a master of developing fictitious informants, sent communiqués to the bureau claiming informant privilege. He wrote in one communiqué that exposure of informants in the SWP case would devastate the informant program. The bureau lied to Judge Griesa when Associate Director James Adams claimed that the FBI pledged confidentiality to informants.

The *Manual of Instructions*, which sets forth investigative procedures for the various classifications of cases, makes no reference to a pledge of confidentiality. On the contrary, the manual states that informants are considered available for interview by departmental attorneys and are available for testimony if needed. The real reason the exposure of informers in the SWP case would be devastating to the FBI is because the FBI had thousands of paper informers so that agents could meet the quota of five each. The FBI could not afford to expose this magnitude of fraud.

"FBI Chicanery" contained page after page of exposure of FBI fraud and corruption. I wrote how the FBI was trying to confuse Judge Griesa by telling him that the exposure of informants would be devastating. When Judge Griesa heard about the documents and my manuscript "FBI Chicanery" having been recovered from the rubble in Jonestown, he ordered the FBI to give him the documents and the manuscript. "FBI Chicanery" was now legally before a judge in a court of law, exactly what Charles Garry had wanted.

When Federal Judge Alfred Kirkland, who was hearing the lawsuit of the Business and Professional People for the Public Interest in Chicago, heard of the raid on Charles Garry's office, he was also interested in getting the information I'd revealed. He ordered the FBI to turn over a copy of everything taken from Garry's office, copies of documents that I had given to the Department of Justice, and a copy of "FBI Chicanery." The FBI told Judge Kirkland that they did not have a copy of "FBI Chicanery," because they had given it to Judge Griesa in New York. The FBI told Kirkland that it would be a violation of my copyright for them to make a copy and give it to Judge Kirkland. The FBI has more jokes to tell federal judges than a one-hour TV comedy show.

When Doug Cassel told me that the FBI did not have a second copy of "FBI Chicanery" to give to Judge Kirkland, I asked, "What about the copy they took from Charles Garry's office?" When Cassel informed Kirkland that the FBI office in San Francisco had a second copy of "FBI Chicanery," the FBI ate crow and sent the manuscript to Kirkland. "FBI Chicanery" was now in the hands of two federal judges, something I had not hoped for in my wildest dreams.

The FBI had stonewalled Judge Kirkland for several years, and Kirkland believed the FBI's motto of fidelity, bravery, and integrity. In January 1979, Judge Kirkland was about to rule in favor of the FBI until Doug Cassel showed him my manuscript on black bag jobs. The FBI had told Congress and Kirkland that only 238 black bag jobs had been conducted nationwide between the years 1942 to 1966 on fourteen targets. In "FBI Chicanery," I had documented at least 500 bag jobs against more than fifty targets in Chicago alone between the years of 1952 and 1957. By the time Judge Kirkland had read through "FBI Chicanery," he decided against the FBI on all twenty-one demands made by the Business and Professional People for the Public Interest.

The FBI admitted in 1981 that there had been at least 500 black bag jobs in the Chicago area directed against approximately fifty targets. The FBI also acknowledged that if the bag jobs were done today, they would be illegal.

When the BPI won their lawsuit against the FBI, Doug Cassel, the general counsel, made a statement to the media. Cassel said, "Without Wes Swearingen, we never would have won the case."

There were several judges who handled the BPI case from its inception to the final consent decree, ruling against the FBI's illegal activities. It was Federal District Judge Susan Getzendanner's ruling that made it illegal for the FBI to do bag jobs in Chicago.* Illegal

---

* The Chicago FBI office is prohibited from maintaining any files on

searches always have been a violation of the Constitution, but now it is a violation of a federal court order, which gives some teeth to the penalties. An illegal search in violation of the Constitution means only that the evidence collected from the illegal search or bag job cannot be used in court. Judge Getzendanner's ruling is of major importance to any FBI agent in Chicago who has a mind set to do a black bag job in the Chicago area, because it means instant prison if he or she is caught. However, the rest of the United States is not covered by Judge Getzendanner's ruling and so citizens should be alert for surreptitious entries by the FBI if they are political activists or environmentalists hoping to protect the country.

Federal Judge John F. Grady heard the case in Chicago brought against the FBI and the Chicago police by the relatives of Black Panther Party members Fred Hampton and Mark Clark, who had been gunned down by the Chicago police on December 4, 1969.

I was scheduled to be a witness for the Panthers' relatives in a second trial, the first having ended in a hung jury. The FBI did not want me on the witness stand and they could not afford to let a copy of "FBI Chicanery" and "Bag Job" appear before another federal judge.

The FBI said that the case would cause hardship to the survivors and that another trial would be expensive to the taxpayers. The FBI was not worried about the expense to taxpayers and they were not concerned with the feelings of the survivors of the Panthers. The FBI was acting to minimize publicity of allegations that it had conspired with the Chicago police to assassinate members of the Black Panther Party.

In November 1982, Judge Grady nevertheless determined that there was sufficient evidence of a conspiracy between the FBI and the Chicago police to deprive Fred Hampton and Mark Clark of their civil rights to award the plaintiffs $1.8 million in damages.

Four years later, Judge Griesa decided in favor of the Socialist Workers Party. The SWP was awarded damages in the amount of

---

individuals if they are targets of illegal surveillance, which effectively covers citizens living within the entire territory covered by the Chicago office, not just within the city limits.

$42,000 relating to disruption activities, $96,500 for the surreptitious entries or bag jobs, and $125,000 for the use of informants, for a total of $246,000. The outcome of the Elmer Geronimo Pratt case is not as happy. The attorneys for Geronimo Pratt had won a hearing before Federal Magistrate Kronenberg in Los Angeles in January 1985. I testified on behalf of Geronimo Pratt but, once again, the FBI and the Los Angeles Police Department displayed their true colors and stonewalled the federal court.

In June 1991, TV Channel 5 in San Francisco, Station KPIX, in their program called "Behind the Headlines," did a story on Pratt and his frame-up by the FBI and the LAPD. Station KPIX asked me by telephone to explain the FBI's actions against Pratt and the Black Panther Party.

I said, "I can't. How do you explain an organization like the FBI putting an innocent man in jail for twenty years or plotting assassinations of people just because they are black or they happen to be charismatic leaders in an organization that you don't like? The FBI didn't end up being any better than the Gestapo. The only thing they had on us were numbers."

In January 1994, FOX News of Los Angeles aired a three-part series on Geronimo Pratt. I appeared on the program in Pratt's defense in the hope that the public would begin to understand what happened to Geronimo Pratt, an innocent man, and would demand that the courts release Pratt and declare him innocent.

On May 24, 1994, the *Los Angeles Times* ran a front-page article on Pratt and the witness against him, Julius Carl Butler, a former FBI informer and now a leader in the First African Methodist Episcopal Church in Los Angeles. The *Los Angeles Times* reporter interviewed me to corroborate some of the details. Julius Butler claims to this day that he was not an FBI informer, but I have seen FBI documents that show Butler was contacted at least thirty-three times over a two-year period, which includes the time just before and just after the Pratt trial. The FBI closed its informant file on Butler during the Pratt trial so that Butler could testify under oath that he was not an FBI informer.

Maybe I am naive, confused, or just stupid. If the FBI had an informant file on Julius Carl Butler for two years, and Butler was contacted every month by an FBI agent for more than two years for a total of at least thirty-three times, how then can the FBI and Butler say Butler was not an informer or a snitch? I think the problem here is that I am not calling Butler by the correct name, and therefore the FBI is denying that he is what he is, a fink. Maybe the FBI calls Butler a "giver of information", therefore in bureau-ese Butler is not an informer.

Butler and the FBI can deny all they want that Butler was an informer, fink, snitch, or whatever, but I have seen the FD-209 Informant Contact forms, and this is the form that we agents used for the twenty-five years I was in the FBI to record contacts with informers.

My struggle to help Elmer Geronimo Pratt gain an unconditional release from prison will not end until the FBI and the Los Angeles courts admit that Pratt was framed for murder.

As for me, I refuse to be intimidated by the FBI's efforts to annoy and harass me. The typewriter that the FBI seized from my boat in 1978 was not returned to me until the fall of 1982, four years later. The FBI refused to return the draft copies of Dave Dellinger's articles for *Seven Days* magazine and the list of informants I had made from the newspapers and from the Congressional Record. The manuscript "Bag Job," which I sent to the FBI in 1981 for their thirty-day approval, was not returned to me until October 1984, three and one-half years later.

Paula and I made three round trips to Hawaii from California. Our last return trip was to San Diego in 1987, where we remained until we sold our boat in 1990 and became landlubbers. The most memorable years of our lives were spent on the open ocean, with the wind and the sea, the flying fish, the playful dolphins, the fantastic sunsets, the ever changing moon, and the trillions of stars on a dark night. We loved the nineteen years we had lived on the water and would not trade them for anything, except maybe for another nineteen years on the water.

All my efforts to expose FBI corruption did attract one particularly annoying act of retribution from the bureau. My former employers showed their true colors by butting in to my personal life. My brother Tom died suddenly in 1987 from cancer of the lymph glands. I had visited with Tom in the summer of 1986, and we had discussed our aging mother Ina, who was then ninety-six. Tom had claimed to be a millionaire several times over and he had said he would take care of Mom until the end. Well, Tom had not made any provision in his will or his multimillion-dollar trust to care for Ina, as he had promised, because he had thought he would outlive her.

Ina was ninety-seven when she filed a lawsuit against Tom's estate in an effort to obtain enough money to keep her comfortable in a convalescent home until she passed away. Charles Garry acted as her attorney as a favor to me.

An attorney by the name of John Babbage, Tom's good friend, attorney, and golfing partner, represented Tom's estate. Tom once had told me that Babbage was an ex-FBI agent. Tom had said that Babbage had been in the FBI for about three years during World War II to avoid the draft. After the war Babbage had resigned from the FBI and joined the Society of Former Agents.

On August 24, 1988, my mother's lawsuit came to trial. The day I testified, who showed up but Mr. Robert H. Matheson, Jr., ex-FBI agent and an officer in the Society of Former Agents of the FBI. Matheson had been the Special Agent in Charge of the Administrative Division in Los Angeles when I had retired, and he is the one who had done my departing interview.

The only way Robert Matheson, Jr. could have known that I was to testify on that day was for John Babbage to have told him. It was obvious that former FBI agents and members of the Society of Former Agents of the FBI had conspired to harass me and my family during such a private and emotional affair. This still outrages me. What right does the FBI or the Society of Former Agents have to interfere in private family matters that have nothing to do with the bureau, the government, or the Society of Former Agents of the FBI?

I congratulate Babbage, Matheson, and those of their ilk for displaying in open court the true motto of the FBI.

The Hoover era will haunt the FBI for decades to come, no matter what historians and critics write, because J. Edgar Hoover and his sycophantic and praetorian associates embarked knowingly on a course to undermine the Constitution and the justice system of the United States.

Abraham Lincoln once said, "Let the people know the truth and the country is safe."

Not until the FBI is forced to tell the truth will the citizens of the United States of America be safe from the national police force the FBI controls and the COINTELPRO it secretly continues to operate.

May God have mercy on those who disbelieve.

A p p e n d i x   A

The Logistics of a Black Bag Job

1. Identify the subject.

2. Determine target's place of employment and type of employment.

3. Identify the mode of transportation.

4. Identify other residents of the household.

5. Determine whether target has any other visitors in the residence such as relatives, maids, etc.

6. Identify the landlord if the residence is not a privately owned home or condominium.

7. Perform a trial run.

8. Start the bag job.

A. All members of the surveillance team, regardless of their position, must be in radio contact with one another or in contact with a reasonable relay. No bag job should start or continue if any member of the team is out of radio contact. A hostile force, such as another member of the organization under investigation, local police, or a thief, may have neutralized one of your teammates and may monitor your movements by radio.

Everyone involved must be physically and mentally alert, aware of their surroundings, attentive and aggressive, and a team player.

The successful execution of a bag job depends upon everyone doing their job correctly. There is no room for error, bad judgment, or heroes. A successfully planned and executed bag job will never give you any surprises that you cannot handle. (A locked door should never be taped open as was done by the infamously incompetent Watergate burglars during the break-in in 1972 at Democratic Party headquarters in Washington, D.C.)

A bag job is a tremendous strain on the nerves. Emotions can run high in these tense situations, and each member of the team must be able to control himself mentally, physically, and emotionally, and have confidence that the others can do likewise.

B. The surveillance team will follow the subject and any members of the residence. Depending upon the persons to be followed, no less than two surveillance agents should be used per person, unless school children are involved, in which case one agent per child will suffice. In the case of very young children, it is sometimes advisable to have two agents so as to avoid the appearance of being a child molester.

C. Once all members of the residence have been surveilled away from the residence or accounted for in another location, and there are no apparent obstacles, then the plan is ready for a trial run.

D. When the "ball players" are ready to begin the "game," those agents designated to telephone the residence of any neighbors in a position to observe the front should place their calls at a precise moment as instructed by the "outside man."

E. The "outside man" or "lookout" will call the "inside team" into position and will alert the various surveillance agents that the "ball players" are approaching the field. The inside team on the trial run will consist of the lock picker and one radio person.

Radio transmissions can be received by anyone with the proper equipment, such as a 200-channel scanning radio, or other similar portable equipment with a retail price of around $300, so communications must be innocuous.

F. The "pickup man" will deliver the inside team to the front door or to the most suitable location to avoid attention; this could be the front door, back door, a nearby alley, or a parking garage. The inside team is dropped off and the "pickup man" departs the immediate area to stand by for further instructions through the outside person or lookout.

G. The "inside team" approaches and examines the entrance for obvious alarm systems. If no alarms are noted, the inside team will make the surreptitious entry into the residence or office. The radio person of the inside team will immediately announce to the outside person that "the players are on the field."

H. The trial run will consist of an immediate search of all rooms for friends, relatives, housekeepers, or anyone associated with the subject to be sure the "field" is clear. The inside team will announce to the outside person some description of the events taking place inside. For example, if a quick observation reveals no information available for future bag jobs, the inside person may announce that the game is being called for lack of interest in today's game or poor attendance.

If prospects look good, the photographer may be called in through some phrase such as, "Send in the press photographer; we may need photographs for a starting line-up for future games."

It is important to keep the surveillance agents advised of events as they happen so that they feel they are part of the action. If the surveillance team does not find out what happened until the end of the day or the next day, morale will suffer and future bag jobs may be compromised because the surveillance team will feel they are not qualified to be kept informed of current events.

If the situation is such that a quick "game" can be played, that is, the bag job can be done with one quick photographic session, the inside person will ask the outside person to check with other players to see if three or four innings can be played.

If the surveillance team has everyone under control, the outside person will announce something like, "Weather permitting, the relief pitchers can go a full nine innings." This alerts the inside team that a regular bag job of one or two hours can be handled by the surveillance team with no problem.

I. Photographs may be needed to rearrange articles after completion of the bag job depending upon the inside condition and the number of records to be examined. A Polaroid camera is ideal for this purpose. Once an examination of the inside layout is clearly in mind and notes have been taken on placement of various articles on the desk, in file cabinets, etc., the ball game can be played.

A progress report from the inside should be given to the outside person every few minutes. When the inside team is through, they will announce the completion by saying something like, "The game is in the bottom of the ninth with two men out and the count is two and two; have the pickup man ready to transport the players back home."

The outside person may then relay the message to all surveillance units that they may, "Head for the barn."

A p p e n d i x   B

Operations Against Leon Katzen

The break-ins and special awards for the operations on Leon Katzen were approved by the following officials:

J. Edgar Hoover, Director
Clyde Tolson, Associate Director
Alan H. Belmont, Assistant Director in Charge, Domestic Security Division
Fred J. Baumgardner, Section Chief, Domestic Security Division
W.R. Glavin, Assistant Director in Charge, Administrative Division
H.L. Edwards, FBI Headquarters
[First name unknown] Wacherman, FBI Headquarters
[First name unknown] Usilton, FBI Headquarters
John F. Malone, Special Agent in Charge, Chicago
Kline Weatherford, Special Agent in Charge, Chicago
W.G. "Guy" Banister, Special Agent in Charge, Chicago
Joseph P. McMahan, Security Coordinator, Chicago
Edward P. Grigalus, Relief Security Coordinator, Chicago
Mauritz E. Gahlon, Supervisor, Chicago
Edwin W. Flint, Supervisor, Chicago
Richard Baker, Relief Supervisor, Chicago, later Special Agent in Charge, Criminal Division II, New York City
Robert J. Wilson, Supervisor, Chicago

A p p e n d i x   C

The Arrest of Claude Lightfoot

Until the arrest of Claude Lightfoot on June 26, 1954, the many long hours of the FBI's physical surveillance on Communist Party members, the legal and illegal bugs, the legal and illegal wiretaps, the legal and illegal mail covers, and the illegal break-ins of offices and bag jobs on residences had not produced a single Communist Party fugitive apprehension in the territory covered by the Chicago office. It was a stroke of luck that led to my arrest of Lightfoot, Chairman of the Communist Party of Illinois and a fugitive, charged with violation of the Smith Act. (See next page for my commendation.)

Two of our surveillance squad and bag job agents were driving home on a Friday night. They lived in the affordable housing area of Hammond, Indiana. The two agents spotted the gray Plymouth that we had surveilled for months, maybe even for years. The car was registered to Sam Kushner, but it was used by countless members of the Communist Party for transportation. We saw it almost daily, but each time it was being driven by a different party member.

When the two agents saw a black man they thought could be Claude Lightfoot in the gray Plymouth driving northbound on the Outer Drive, they made an illegal U-turn across the median, and followed the Plymouth to a black neighborhood on Chicago's South Side. The unknown driver evaded the impromptu surveillance near Stoney Island Avenue.

The next day, Saturday, the entire security division of the Chicago office, consisting of at least 125 agents, was called out to search the South Side of Chicago. We were paired off and assigned

OFFICE OF THE DIRECTOR

UNITED STATES DEPARTMENT OF JUSTICE

FEDERAL BUREAU OF INVESTIGATION

WASHINGTON 25, D. C.

July 23, 1954

Personal and Confidential

Mr. M. Wesley Swearingen
Federal Bureau of Investigation
Chicago, Illinois

Dear Mr. Swearingen:

You are to be commended for your
excellent participation in the investigation
and apprehension of Claude Mack Lightfoot,
Smith Act subject.

Your sincere and conscientious
application to your assignment, particularly
in the difficult identification of the subject,
is most gratifying to me. I want you to know
of my appreciation for the very successful
results achieved.

Sincerely yours,

J. Edgar Hoover

The commendation I received for my arrest of Claude Lightfoot.

to grids or quadrants to search until we found the gray Plymouth. We drove up and down the alleys and side streets. It took about an hour or so to find the gray Plymouth parked on a street in an all-black neighborhood.

It was a hot, sunny day, and so *Sam McGiver* and I, the two youngest agents on the squad, volunteered to sit in the unventilated panel truck to observe the Plymouth. We were driven into position and we waited all afternoon. It was so hot inside the truck that we had to strip to our shorts and we were soaking wet from perspiration. I had worked in the Weirton Steel Mill, in high school, where temperatures were 180 degrees near the annealing furnaces. The inside of the truck was about 145 degrees. I radioed to our supervisor Bob Wilson that we could not take the temperature much longer without becoming corpses.

When Bob Wilson opened the panel truck door and climbed inside, the heat forced him back onto the street. Bob drove us to a neighborhood gas station where we drank water and cooled off. Just then, the surveillance team spotted a black man entering the Plymouth and driving to a housing project.

Bob drove us to the housing project and I saw several FBI agents surrounding Claude Lightfoot. None of the other agents had ever seen Claude Lightfoot so they were afraid to identify themselves. I walked up and asked, "What's going on?"

Claude turned to me and said, "These guys said that I look like somebody who just left an apartment where there was a burglary."

I couldn't believe the agents' stupidity. I pulled out my credentials and said, "Claude, I am Special Agent M. Wesley Swearingen of the FBI. You are under arrest for violation of the Smith Act of 1940."

Lightfoot just kind of wilted. I handcuffed him and marched him off to a waiting car and took him to the FBI office on the nineteenth floor of the old Bankers Building.

A p p e n d i x D

Hoover's Commendation

OFFICE OF THE DIRECTOR

UNITED STATES DEPARTMENT OF JUSTICE
FEDERAL BUREAU OF INVESTIGATION

WASHINGTON 25, D. C.

October 5, 1955

Personal and Confidential

Mr. M. Wesley Swearingen
Federal Bureau of Investigation
Chicago, Illinois

Dear Mr. Swearingen:

I am happy to take this opportunity to
advise you of the approval of a cash award for
you in the amount of $150.00 in recognition of
your outstanding participation in the development
of a number of highly confidential sources of information relative to the internal security of the
country. You will be forwarded a check for this
amount, less withholding tax, in the near future.

You displayed notable determination and
unusual perseverance in overcoming the many diffi-
culties inherent in operations such as these and
through your diligent efforts success was realized.
Your extremely fine performance indeed merits praise
and commendation.

Sincerely yours,

J. Edgar Hoover

Notes to Foreword

1. On the Media break-in and ensuing events, see Ward Churchill and Jim Vander Wall, *The COINTELPRO Papers: Documents from the FBI's Secret Wars Against Dissent in the United States* (Boston: South End Press, 1990), pp. 332-333.

2. U.S. Senate, Select Committee to Study Government Operations with Respect to Intelligence Activities, *Hearings on Intelligence Activities, Vol. 6: The Federal Bureau of Investigation* (Washington, D.C.: 94th Cong., 1st Sess., U.S. Government Printing Office, 1975); *Final Report: Supplementary Detailed Staff Reports on Intelligence Activities and the Rights of Americans, Book III* (Washington, D.C.: 94th Cong., 2nd Sess., U.S. Government Printing Office, 1976). Also see U.S. Senate, Committee on the Judiciary, Subcommittee on Constitutional Rights, *Hearings on FBI Counterintelligence Programs* (Washington, D.C.: 93rd Cong., 2nd Sess., U.S. Government Printing Office, 1974).

3. Robert Justin Goldstein, *Political Repression in Modern America, 1870 to the Present* (Cambridge/London: Schenckman Books/Two Continents Publishing Group, 1978); Cathy Perkus, ed., *COINTELPRO: The FBI's Secret War on Political Freedom* (New York: Monad Press, 1975); Athan Theoharis, *Spying on Americans: Political Surveillance from Hoover to the Huston Plan* (Philadelphia: Temple University Press, 1978); David Wise, *The American Police State: The Government Against the People* (New York: Vintage Books, 1976); Peter Matthiessen, *In the Spirit of Crazy Horse* (New York: Viking Press, 1983); Brian Glick, *War at Home: Covert Action Against U.S. Activists and What We Can Do About It* (Boston: South End Press, 1989); David J. Garrow, *The FBI and Martin Luther King, Jr.: From "Solo" to Memphis* (New York: W.W. Norton, 1981); Ross Gelbspan, *Break-ins, Death Threats and the FBI: The Covert War Against the Central America Movement* (Boston: South End Press, 1991); Ward Churchill and Jim VanderWall, *Agents of Repression: The FBI's Secret Wars Against the Black Panther Party and the American Indian Movement*; and *The COINTELPRO Papers, op. cit.*

4. See *Political Repression in Modern America, op. cit.*; *Break-Ins, Death Threats and the FBI, op. cit.*; *The COINTELPRO Papers, op. cit.* Also see U.S. House of Representatives, Committee on the Judiciary, Subcommittee on Civil and Constitutional Rights, *Break-ins at Sanctuary Churches and Organizations Opposed to Administration Policy in Central America* (Washington, D.C.: 100th Cong., 1st Sess., U.S. Government Printing Office, 1988); *CISPES and FBI Counter-Terrorism Investigations* (Washington, D.C., 100th Cong., 2d Sess., U.S. Government Printing Office, 1988).

5. For a thorough delineation of the FBI's standard arsenal of domestic counterintelligence (COINTELPRO) techniques, see *Agents of Repression, op. cit.*, pp. 37-53.

6. With regard to official material, see, e.g., U.S. Senate, Select Committee to Study Government Operations with Respect to Intelligence Activities, *Final Report: Foreign and Military Intelligence, Book I* (Washington, D.C.: 94th Cong., 2d Sess., U.S. Government Printing Office, 1976); *Final Report: Supplementary Detailed Staff Reports on Intelligence and Military Intelligence, Book IV* (Washington, D.C.: 95th Cong., 1st Sess., U.S. Government Printing Office, 1977). Also see the material compiled by the Church Committee for broader consumption under the title *Alleged Assassination Plots Involving Foreign Leaders: Interim Report of the Senate Select Committee to Study Government Operations with Respect to Intelligence Activities* (New York: W.W. Norton, 1976). Any sample of excellent unofficial sources must include Philip Agee and Louis Wolf, eds., *Dirty Work: The CIA in Western Europe* (Syracuse, NY: Lyle Stuart, 1978); Ellen Ray, William Schapp, Karl Van Meter and Louis Wolf, eds., *Dirty Work 2: The CIA in Africa* (Syracuse, NY: Lyle Stuart, 1979); William Blum, *The CIA: A Forgotten History* (London: Zed Press, 1986); John Ranelagh, *The Agency: The Rise and Decline of the CIA* (New York: Touchstone Books, 1986).

7. Philip Agee, *Inside the Company: A CIA Diary* (New York: Penguin Books, 1975); John Stockwell, *In Search of Enemies: A CIA Story* (New York: W.W. Norton, 1978); Frank Snepp, *Decent Interval: An Insider's Account of Saigon's Indecent End Told by the CIA's Chief Strategy Analyst in Vietnam* (New York: Vintage

Books, 1978); Victor D. Marchetti and John D. Marks, *The CIA and the Cult of Intelligence* (New York: Laurel Publishers, 1980); Ralph W. McGehee, *Deadly Deceits: My 25 Years in the CIA* (New York: Sheridan Square, 1983).

8. Joseph L. Schott, *No Left Turns: The FBI in Peace and War* (New York: Praeger, 1975).

9. William Turner, *Hoover's FBI: The Men and the Myth* (New York: Dell, 1971).

10. For details on Pratt's imprisonment and the Hampton/Clark assassinations, see *Agents of Repression, op. cit.*, pp. 64-94.

11. See *The COINTELPRO Papers, op. cit.*, pp. 214-219, 271-298. On Peltier, also see *In the Spirit of Crazy Horse, op. cit.*; *Agents of Repression, op. cit.*; and Jim Messerschmidt, *The Trial of Leonard Peltier* (Boston: South End Press, 1982).

12. *Inside the Company, op. cit.*; *In Search of Enemies, op. cit.*

13. For further information on several of these matters, see Jo Durden-Smith, *Who Killed George Jackson? Fantasies, Paranoia, and the Revolution* (New York: Alfred A. Knopf, 1976).

14. *Ibid.* Also see Gregory Jackson, *The Dragon Has Come* (New York: Harper & Row, 1974).

15. See generally, U.S. Senate, Select Committee to Study Government Operations with Respect to Intelligence Activities, *The FBI's Covert Program to Destroy the Black Panther Party* (Washington, D.C.: 94th Cong., 2nd Sess., U.S. Government Printing Office, 1976).

16. Patricia King, "A Snitch's Tale: The Killer Gang (An Informer Tells About Life as an 'El Rukn')," *Newsweek*, November 6, 1989.

17. Swearingen's thinking on the matter, whatever it is, might well have complemented existing theses, such as those elaborated by Alfred W. McCoy in his *The Politics of Heroin: CIA Complicity in the Global Drug Trade* (New York: Lawrence Hill Books, 1991), and Peter Dale Scott and Jonathan Marshall in their *Cocaine Politics: Drugs, Armies, and the CIA in Central America* (Berkeley: University of California Press, 1991).

Index

About South End Press

South End Press is a non-profit, collectively run book publisher with over 180 titles in print. Since our founding in 1977, we have tried to meet the needs of readers who are exploring, or are already committed to, the politics of radical social change.

Our goal is to publish books that encourage critical thinking and constructive action on the key political, cultural, social, economic, and ecological issues shaping life in the United States and in the world. In this way, we hope to give expression to a wide diversity of democratic social movements and to provide an alternative to the products of corporate publishing.

Through the Institute for Social and Cultural Change, South End Press works with other political media projects—Z Magazine; Speak Out!, a speakers bureau; the New Liberation News Service; and the Publishers Support Project—to expand access to information and critical analysis. If you would like a free catalog of South End Press books or information about our membership program, which offers two free books and a 40 percent discount on all titles, please write to us at: South End Press, 116 Saint Botolph Street, Boston, MA 02115.

Other South End Press Titles of Interest

Too Close for Comfort: The Fascist Potential of the U.S. Right
by Chip Berlet and Matthew Lyons

COINTELPRO Papers: Documents from the FBI's Secret Wars Against Dissent in the United States
by Ward Churchill and Jim Vander Wall

Agents of Repression: The FBI's Secret Wars Against the American Indian Movement and the Black Panther Party
by Ward Churchill and Jim Vander Wall

The Trial of Leonard Peltier
by Jim Messerschmidt

About the Author

M. Wesley Swearingen was a FBI agent for twenty-five years. Since retiring he has been instrumental in documenting FBI harassment of political dissidents. He lives in Arizona.